French
phrase book

AA Publishing

Contents

English edition prepared by First Edition Translations Ltd, Great Britain
Designed and produced by AA Publishing

First published in 1992 as Wat & Hoe Frans,
© Uitgeverij Kosmos bv - Utrecht/Antwerpen
Van Dale Lexicografie bv - Utrecht/Antwerpen

This edition © Automobile Association Developments Limited 1997
Reprinted Jun and Sep 1998
Reprinted Oct 1999
Reprinted Feb and Sep 2000
Reprinted Apr and Sep 2001
Reprinted Feb and Aug 2002
Reprinted Feb 2003, Jul 2003 and Sep 2003
Reprinted Dec 2003

A CIP catalogue record for this book is available from the
British Library

Published by AA Publishing (a trading name of Automobile Association
Developments Limited, whose registered office is Millstream,
Maidenhead Road, Windsor, Berkshire SL4 5GD Registered number
1878835).

A01978

Typeset by Anton Graphics Ltd, Andover, Hampshire.

Printed and bound in Italy by Printer Trento srl.

Find out more about AA Publishing and the wide range of services the
AA provides by visiting our web site at www.theAA.com

Introduction

● **Welcome to the AA's French Phrasebook, which contains everything you'd expect from a comprehensive language guide. It's concise, accessible and easy to understand, and you'll find it indispensable on your trip abroad.**

This guide is divided into 15 themed sections and starts with a pronunciation table which explains the phonetic pronunciation to all the words and phrases you'll need to know for your trip, while at the back of the book is an extensive word list and grammar guide which will help you construct basic sentences in French.

Throughout the book you'll come across coloured boxes with a 🌑 beside them. These are designed to help you if you can't understand what your listener is saying to you. Hand the book over to them and encourage them to point to the appropriate answer to the question you are asking.

Other coloured boxes in the book - this time without the symbol - give alphabetical listings of themed words with their English translations beside them.

For extra clarity, we have put all English words and phrases in black, foreign language terms in red and their phonetic pronunciation in italic.

This phrasebook covers all subjects you are likely to come across during the course of your visit, from reserving a room for the night to ordering food and drink at a restaurant and what to do if your car breaks down or you lose your traveller's cheques and money. With over 2,000 commonly used words and essential phrases at your fingertips you can rest assured that you will be able to get by in all situations, so let the AA's French Phrasebook become your passport to a secure and enjoyable trip!

Pronunciation guide

The pronunciation provided should be read as if it were English, bearing in mind the following main points:

Vowels

a, à or â	a in man	ah	table	tahbl
é	like a in make	ay	été	aytay
è, ê, e	like ai in air	eh	rêve	rehv
e	sometimes like u in fluff	uh	le, ne, je, me	luh, nuh, jhuh, muh
i	like ee in seen	ee	si	see
ô	like o in foam	oa	hôtel	oatehl
o	like o in John	o	homme	om
	sometimes like ô	oa	arroser	ahroasay
u	between ee and ew	ew	tu	tew

Combinations of letters which represent vowel sounds:

ez, er	similar to é	ay	louer	looay
ais, ait	the eh sound	eh	fait	feh
au, eau	similar to ô	oa	beau	boa
ail	like i in side	ahy	travail	trahvahy
ei	similar to è	eh	Seine	sehn
eille	eh + y as in yes	ehy	bouteille	bootehy
eu	similar to e above	uh	feu	fuh
iè	ye as in yes	yeh	siècle	syehkl
ié, ier, iez	y + the ay sound	yay	janvier	jhohnvyay
ille	ee + y as in yes	eey	famille	fameey
oi, oy	combines w + a	wah	moi	mwah
ou, oû	oo as in hoot	oo	vous	voo
ui	combines w and ee	wee	cuir	kweer

Consonants

ch	like sh in shine	sh	chaud	shoa
ç	like s in some	s	garçon	gahrsawn
g	before e, i and y like s in leisure	jh	nager	nahjhay
	before a, o and u like g in got	g	gâteau	gahtoa
gn	like ny in canyon	ny	agneau	ahnyoa
h	silent			
j	like s in leisure	jh	jour	jhoor
qu	like k in kind	k	que	kuh
r	rolled at the back of the throat			
w	like v in vine	v	wagonlit	vahgawnlee

Nasal sounds

Nasal sounds are written in French by adding an n to a vowel or a combination of vowels pronounced as the English ng:

an/am, en/em	a little like song	ohn	français, lentement	frohnseh, lohntmohn
in/im, ain, aim, ein	a little like bang	ahn	instant, faim	ahnstohn, fahn
on/om	a nasal form of awn	awn	non	nawn
un/um	a little like rung	uhn	un	uhn
ien	y + the ahn sound	yahn	bien	byahn

Useful lists

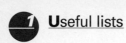

Useful lists

1.1 Today or tomorrow?

What day is it today?	C'est quel jour aujourd'hui?
	seh kehl jhoor oajhoordwee?
Today's Monday	Aujourd'hui c'est lundi
	oajhoordwee seh luhndee
– Tuesday	Aujourd'hui c'est mardi
	oajhoordwee seh mahrdee
– Wednesday	Aujourd'hui c'est mercredi
	oajhoordwee seh mehrkruhdee
– Thursday	Aujourd'hui c'est jeudi
	oajhoordwee seh jhuhdee
– Friday	Aujourd'hui c'est vendredi
	oajhoordwee seh vohndruhdee
– Saturday	Aujourd'hui c'est samedi
	oajhoordwee seh sahmdee
– Sunday	Aujourd'hui c'est dimanche
	oajhoordwee seh deemohnsh
in January	en janvier
	ohn jhohnvyay
since February	depuis février
	duhpwee fayvryay
in spring	au printemps
	oa prahntohn
in summer	en été; l'été
	ohn naytay; laytay
in autumn	en automne
	ohn noatonn
in winter	en hiver; l'hiver
	ohn neevehr; leevehr
1998	mille neuf cent quatre-vingt-dix-huit
	meel nuhf sohn kahtr vahn dee zweet
the twentieth century	le vingtième siècle
	luh vahntyehm syehkl
What's the date today?	Quelle est la date aujourd'hui?
	kehl eh lah daht oajhoordwee?
Today's the 24th	Aujourd'hui on est le vingt-quatre
	oajhoordwee awn neh luh vahnkahtr
Monday 3 November 1997	lundi, le trois novembre 1997
	luhndee, luh trwah novohnbr meel nuhf sohn kahtr vahn dee seht
in the morning	le matin
	luh mahtahn
in the afternoon	l'après-midi
	lahpreh meedee
in the evening	le soir
	luh swahr
at night	la nuit
	lah nwee
this morning	ce matin
	suh mahtahn
this afternoon	cet après-midi
	seht ahpreh meedee

this evening _____	ce soir
	suh swahr
tonight _____	ce soir
	suh swahr
last night _____	hier soir
	yehr swahr
this week _____	cette semaine
	seht suhmehn
next month _____	le mois prochain
	luh mwah proshahn
last year _____	l'année passée
	lahnay pahsay
next... _____	prochain/prochaine
	proshahn/proshehn
in...days/weeks/ _____	dans...jours/semaines/mois/ans
months/years	*dohn...jhoor/suhmehn/mwah/ohn*
...weeks ago _____	il y a...semaines
	eel ee ah...suhmehn
day off _____	jour de congé
	jhoor duh kawnjhay

🕐 .2 Bank holidays

● **The most important** Bank holidays in France are the following:

January 1	Le Jour de l'An (New Year's Day)
March/April	Pâques, (Easter)
	le lundi de Pâques (Easter Monday)
May 1	La Fête du Travail (May Day; Labour Day)
May 8	Le Jour de la Libération (Liberation Day)
May/June	L'Ascension; la Pentecôte (Ascension; Whit Sunday)
July 14	La Fête Nationale (Bastille Day)
August 15	L'Assomption (Assumption)
November 1	La Toussaint (All Saints' Day)
November 11	L'Armistice (Armistice Day)
December 25	Noël (Christmas)

Most shops, banks and government institutions are closed on these days. Banks close the afternoon before a Bank holiday and some banks close on Mondays in the provinces. Good Friday and Boxing Day are not Bank Holidays.

🕐 .3 What time is it?

What time is it? _____	Quelle heure est-il?
	kehl uhr eh teel?
It's nine o'clock _____	Il est neuf heures
	eel eh nuh vuhr
– five past ten_____	Il est dix heures cinq
	eel eh dee zuhr sahnk
– a quarter past eleven ____	Il est onze heures et quart
	eel eh tawnz uhr ay kahr
– twenty past twelve_____	Il est douze heures vingt
	eel eh dooz uhr vahn
– half past one _____	Il est une heure et demie
	eel eh tewn uhr ay duhmee
– twenty–five to three_____	Il est trois heures moins vingt-cinq
	eel eh trwah zuhr mwahn vahn sahnk

– a quarter to four	Il est quatre heures moins le quart	
	eel eh kahtr uhr mwahn luh kahr	
– ten to five	Il est cinq heures moins dix	
	eel eh sahnk uhr mwahn dees	
– twelve noon	Il est midi	
	eel eh meedee	
– midnight	Il est minuit	
	eel eh meenwee	
half an hour	une demi-heure	
	ewn duhmee uhr	
What time?	A quelle heure?	
	ah kehl uhr?	
What time can I come round?	A quelle heure puis-je venir?	
	ah kehl uhr pwee jhuh vuhneer?	
At...	A...	
	ah...	
After...	Après...	
	ahpreh...	
Before...	Avant...	
	ahvohn...	
Between...and...	Entre...et...	
	ohntr...ay...	
From...to...	De...à...	
	duh...ah...	
In...minutes	Dans...minutes	
	dohn...meenewt	
– an hour	Dans une heure	
	dohn zewn uhr	
– ...hours	Dans...heures	
	dohn...uhr	
– a quarter of an hour	Dans un quart d'heure	
	dohn zuhn kahr duhr	
– three quarters of an hour	Dans trois quarts d'heure	
	dohn trwah kahr duhr	
early/late	trop tôt/tard	
	troa toa/tahr	
on time	à temps	
	ah tohn	
summertime	l'heure d'été	
	luhr daytay	
wintertime	l'heure d'hiver	
	luhr deevehr	

1.4 One, two, three...

0	zéro	*zayroa*
1	un	*uhn*
2	deux	*duh*
3	trois	*trwah*
4	quatre	*kahtr*
5	cinq	*sahnk*
6	six	*sees*
7	sept	*seht*
8	huit	*weet*
9	neuf	*nuhf*
10	dix	*dees*

11 _____	onze	*awnz*
12 _____	douze	*dooz*
13 _____	treize	*trehz*
14 _____	quatorze	*kahtorz*
15 _____	quinze	*kahnz*
16 _____	seize	*sehz*
17 _____	dix-sept	*dee seht*
18 _____	dix-huit	*dee zweet*
19 _____	dix-neuf	*deez nuhf*
20 _____	vingt	*vahn*
21 _____	vingt et un	*vahn tay uhn*
22 _____	vingt-deux	*vahn duh*
30 _____	trente	*trohnt*
31 _____	trente et un	*trohn tay uhn*
32 _____	trente-deux	*trohnt duh*
40 _____	quarante	*kahrohnt*
50 _____	cinquante	*sahnkohnt*
60 _____	soixante	*swahssohnt*
70 _____	soixante-dix	*swahssohnt dees*
80 _____	quatre-vingts	*kahtr vahn*
90 _____	quatre-vingt-dix	*kahtr vahn dees*
100 _____	cent	*sohn*
101 _____	cent un	*sohn uhn*
110 _____	cent dix	*sohn dees*
120 _____	cent vingt	*sohn vahn*
200 _____	deux cents	*duh sohn*
300 _____	trois cents	*trwah sohn*
400 _____	quatre cents	*kahtr sohn*
500 _____	cinq cents	*sahnk sohn*
600 _____	six cents	*see sohn*
700 _____	sept cents	*seht sohn*
800 _____	huit cents	*wec sohn*
900 _____	neuf cents	*nuhf sohn*
1,000 _____	mille	*meel*
1,100 _____	mille cent	*meel sohn*
2,000 _____	deux mille	*duh meel*
10,000 _____	dix mille	*dee meel*
100,000 _____	cent mille	*sohn meel*
1,000,000 _____	un million	*uhn meelyawn*
1st _____	le premier	*luh pruhmyay*
2nd _____	le deuxième	*luh duhzyehm*
3rd _____	le troisième	*luh trwahzyehm*
4th _____	le quatrième	*luh kahtryehm*
5th _____	le cinquième	*luh sahnkyehm*
6th _____	le sixième	*luh seezyehm*
7th _____	le septième	*luh sehtyehm*
8th _____	le huitième	*luh weetyehm*
9th _____	le neuvième	*luh nuhvyehm*
10th _____	le dixième	*luh deezyehm*
11th _____	le onzième	*luh awnzyehm*
12th _____	le douzième	*luh doozyehm*
13th _____	le treizième	*luh trehzyehm*
14th _____	le quatorzième	*luh kahtorzyehm*
15th _____	le quinzième	*luh kahnzyehm*

16th _____	le seizième	*luh sehzyehm*
17th _____	le dix-septième	*luh dee sehtyehm*
18th _____	le dix-huitième	*luh dee zweetyehm*
19th _____	le dix-neuvième	*luh deez nuhvyehm*
20th _____	le vingtième	*luh vahntyehm*
21st _____	le vingt et unième	*luh vahn tay-ewnyehm*
22nd _____	le vingt-deuxième	*luh vahn duhzyehm*
30th _____	le trentième	*luh trohntyehm*
100th _____	le centième	*luh sohntyehm*
1,000th _____	le millième	*luh meelyehm*

once _____	une fois	*ewn fwah*
twice _____	deux fois	*duh fwah*
double _____	le double	*luh doobl*
triple _____	le triple	*luh treepl*
half _____	la moitié	*lah mwahtyay*
a quarter _____	un quart	*uhn kahr*
a third _____	un tiers	*uhn tyehr*

a couple, a few, some _____	quelques, un nombre de, quelques	
	kehlkuh, uhn nawnbr duh, kehlkuh	
2 + 4 = 6 _____	deux plus quatre égalent six	
	duh plews kahtr aygahl sees	
4 - 2 = 2 _____	quatre moins deux égalent deux	
	kahtr mwahn duh aygahl duh	
2 x 4 = 8 _____	deux fois quatre égalent huit	
	duh fwah kahtr aygahl weet	
4 ÷ 2 = 2 _____	quatre divisé par deux égalent deux	
	kahtr deeveezay pahr duh aygahl duh	
odd/even _____	impair/pair	
	ahnpehr/pehr	
total _____	(au) total	
	(oa) totahl	
6 x 9 _____	six fois neuf	
	see fwah nuhf	

🕐 .5 The weather

Is the weather going to be good/bad?	Va-t-il faire beau/mauvais?
	vah teel fehr boa/moaveh?
Is it going to get colder/hotter?	Va-t-il faire plus froid/plus chaud?
	vah teel fehr plew frwah/plew shoa?
What temperature is it going to be?	Quelle température va-t-il faire?
	Kehl tohnpayrahtewr vah teel fehr?
Is it going to rain?	Va-t-il pleuvoir?
	vah teel pluhvwahr?
Is there going to be a storm?	Va-t-il faire de la tempête?
	vah teel fehr duh lah tohnpeht?
Is it going to snow?	Va-t-il neiger?
	vah teel nehjhay?
Is it going to freeze?	Va-t-il geler?
	vah teel jhuhlay?
Is the thaw setting in?	Va-t-il dégeler?
	vah teel dayjhuhlay?
Is it going to be foggy?	Y aura-t-il du brouillard?
	ee oarah teel dew brooy-yahr?

Is there going to be a _____ thunderstorm?	Va-t-il faire de l'orage? *vah teel fehr duh lorahjh?*
The weather's _____ changing	Le temps change *luh tohn shohnjh*
It's cooling down _____	Ça se rafraîchit *sah suh rahfrehshee*
What's the weather _____ going to be like today/ tomorrow?	Quel temps va-t-il faire aujourd'hui/demain? *kehl tohn vah teel fehr oajhoordwee/duhmahn?*

nuageux cloudy	pluvieux raining	les rafales de vent squalls
beau fine	la canicule scorching hot	l'ouragan (m.) hurricane
chaud hot	la grêle hail	lourd muggy
...degrés (au-dessous/au-dessus de zéro) ...degrees (below/ above zero)	la neige snow	l'orage (m.) thunderstorm
	la pluie rain	orageux stormy
couvert overcast	la vague de chaleur heatwave	pénétrant bleak
le crachin drizzle	l'averse (f.) shower	ciel dégagé clear
doux mild	le brouillard fog	brumeux misty
ensoleillé sunny	le gel ice	vent faible/ modéré/fort light/moderate/ strong wind
frais chilly	le vent wind	
froid cold	le verglas black ice	venteux windy
humide damp	les nuages clouds	

.6 **H**ere, there...

See also 5.1 Asking for directions

here/there _____	ici/là *eesee/lah*
somewhere/nowhere _____	quelque part/nulle part *kehlkuh pahr/newl pahr*
everywhere _____	partout *pahrtoo*
far away/nearby _____	loin/à côté *lwahn/ah koatay*
right/left _____	la droite/la gauche *lah drwaht/lah goash*
to the right/left of _____	à droite de/à gauche de *ah drwaht duh/ah goash duh*
straight ahead _____	tout droit *too drwah*

via	par	*pahr*
in	dans	*dohn*
on	sur	*sewr*
under	sous	*soo*
against	contre	*kawntr*
opposite	en face de	*ohn fahs duh*
next to	à côté de	*ah koatay duh*
near	près de	*preh duh*
in front of	devant	*devohn*
in the centre	au milieu de	*oa meelyuh duh*
forward	en avant	*ohn nahvohn*
down	en bas	*ohn bah*
up	en haut	*ohn oa*
inside	à l'intérieur	*ah lahntayryuhr*
outside	à l'extérieur	*ah lehxtayryuhr*
behind	derrière	*dehryehr*
at the front	à l'avant	*ah lahvohn*
at the back	à l'arrière	*ah lahryehr*
in the north	au nord	*oa nor*
to the south	vers le sud	*vehr luh sewd*
from the west	venant de l'ouest	*vuhnohn duh lwehst*
from the east	venant de l'est	*vuhnohn duh lehst*

.7 What does that sign say?

See 5.4 Traffic signs

à louer	entrée gratuite	ne pas déranger s'il
for hire	admission free	vous plaît
à vendre	entrée interdite	do not disturb please
for sale	no entry	ouvert/fermé
accueil	escalier roulant	open/closed
reception	escalator	peinture fraîche
animaux interdits	escalier	wet paint
no pets allowed	stairs	pelouse interdite
ascenseur	escalier de secours	keep off the grass
lift	fire escape	premiers soins
attention à la marche	...étage	first aid
mind the step	...floor	propriété privée
attention chien	frein de secours	private (property)
méchant	emergency brake	renseignements
beware of the dog	haute tension	information
caisse	high voltage	réservé
pay here	heures d'ouverture	reserved
complet	opening hours	risque d'incendie
full	interdit d'allumer un	fire hazard
dames	feu	soldes
ladies	no open fires	sale
danger	interdit de fumer	sortie
danger	no smoking	exit
défense de toucher	interdit de	sortie de secours
please do not touch	photographier	emergency exit
eau non potable	no photographs	pousser/tirer
no drinking water	liquidation de stock	push/pull
en panne	closing-down sale	toilettes, wc
out of order	messieurs	toilets
entrée	gents/gentlemen	
entrance		

.8 Telephone alphabet

a	ah	comme Anatole	kom ahnnahtol
b	bay	comme Berthe	kom behrt
c	say	comme Célestin	kom saylehstahn
d	day	comme Désiré	kom dayzeeray
e	uh	comme Eugène	kom uhjhehn
f	ehf	comme François	kom frohnswah
g	jhay	comme Gaston	kom gahstawn
h	ash	comme Henri	kom ohnree
i	ee	comme Irma	kom eermah
j	jhee	comme Joseph	kom jhosehf
k	kah	comme Kléber	kom klaybehr
l	ehl	comme Louis	kom looee
m	ehm	comme Marcel	kom mahrsehl
n	ehn	comme Nicolas	kom neekolah
o	oh	comme Oscar	kom oskahr
p	pay	comme Pierre	kom pyehr
q	kew	comme Quintal	kom kahntahl

Useful lists

r_____	*ehr*	comme Raoul	*kom rahool*
s_____	*ehs*	comme Suzanne	*kom sewzahnn*
t_____	*tay*	comme Thérèse	*kom tayrehz*
u_____	*ew*	comme Ursule	*kom ewrsewl*
v_____	*vee*	comme Victor	*kom veektor*
w_____	*doobluhvay*	comme William	*kom weelyahm*
x_____	*eex*	comme Xavier	*kom gsahvyay*
y_____	*eegrehk*	comme Yvonne	*kom eevon*
z_____	*zehd*	comme Zoé	*kom zoa-ay*

🎯 .9 Personal details

surname_____ nom
nawn

christian name(s)_____ prénom(s)
praynawn

initials_____ initiales
eeneesyahl

address (street/number) ___ adresse (rue/numéro)
ahdrehs (rew/newmayroa)

post code/town _____ code postal/ville
kod postahl/veel

sex (male/female) _____ sexe (m/f)
sehx (ehm/ehf)

nationality_____ nationalité
nahsyonahleetay

date of birth _____ date de naissance
daht duh nehsohns

place of birth _____ lieu de naissance
lyuh duh nehsohns

occupation_____ profession
profehsyawn

married/single/divorced____ marié(e) /célibataire/divorcé(e)
mahreeay/sayleebahtehr/deevorsay

widowed _____ veuf/veuve
vuhf/vuhv

(number of) children _____ (nombre d')enfants
(nawnbr d)ohnfohn

identity card/passport/_____ numéro de carte d'identité/
  driving licence number passeport/permis de conduire
newmayroa duh kahrt deedohnteetay/
pahspor/pehrmee duh kawndweer

place and date of issue ___ lieu et date de délivrance
lyuh ay daht duh dayleevrohns

Courtesies

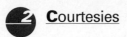

Courtesies

● **It is usual in France** to shake hands on meeting and parting company. Female friends and relatives may kiss each other on both cheeks when meeting and parting company. With men this varies according to the region. It is also polite to say monsieur and madame quite systematically as part of a greeting, i.e. Bonjour, monsieur; au revoir, madame.

● **The English** 'you' is expressed in French by either 'tu' or 'vous'. 'Tu' is the more familiar form of address, used to talk to someone close or used between young people or when adults are talking to young children. 'Vous' is the more formal and polite form of address. 'On' is the generalised form of 'nous' meaning people in general ('one' and 'we' in English).

.1 Greetings

Hello, Mr Smith _____ Bonjour monsieur Smith
bawnjhoor muhsyuh dewpawn

Hello, Mrs Jones _____ Bonjour madame Jones
bawnjhoor mahdahm dewrohn

Hello, Peter _____ Salut, Pierre
sahlew, pyehr

Hi, Helen _____ Ça va, Hélène?
sah vah, aylehn?

Good morning, madam ____ Bonjour madame
bawnjhoor mahdahm

Good afternoon, sir _____ Bonjour monsieur
bawnjhoor muhsyuh

Good evening_____ Bonsoir
bawhnswahr

How are you? _____ Comment allez-vous?
komohn tahlay voo?

Fine, thank you, _____ Très bien et vous?
and you? *treh byahn ay voo?*

Very well _____ Très bien
treh byahn

Not very well _____ Pas très bien
pah treh byahn

Not too bad_____ Ça va
sah vah

I'd better be going_____ Je m'en vais
jhuh mohn veh

I have to be going _____ Je dois partir
jhuh dwah pahrteer

Someone's waiting _____ On m'attend
for me *awn mahtohn*

Bye!_____ Salut!
sahlew!

Goodbye _____ Au revoir
oa ruhvwahr

See you soon _____ A bientôt
ah byahntoa

See you later _____ A tout à l'heure
ah too tah luhr

See you in a little while ____	A tout de suite
	ah toot sweet
Sleep well _____	Dormez bien/dors bien
	dormay byahn, dor byahn
Good night _____	Bonne nuit
	bon nwee
Have fun_____	Amuse-toi bien
	ahmewz twah byahn
Good luck _____	Bonne chance
	bon shahns
Have a nice holiday _____	Bonnes vacances
	bon vahkohns
Have a good trip _____	Bon voyage
	bawn vwahyahjh
Thank you, you too_____	Merci, de même
	mehrsee, duh mehm
Say hello to...for me_____	Mes amitiés à...
	may zahmeetyay ah...

2 .2 How to ask a question

Who?_____	Qui?
	kee?
Who's that? _____	Qui est-ce?
	kee ehs?
What? _____	Quoi?
	kwah?
What's there to_____	Qu'est-ce qu'on peut voir ici?
see here?	*kehsk awn puh vwahr eesee?*
What kind of hotel_____	C'est quelle sorte d'hôtel?
is that?	*seh kehl sort doatehl?*
Where?_____	Où?
	oo?
Where's the toilet? _____	Où sont les toilettes?
	oo sawn lay twahleht?
Where are you going? _____	Où allez-vous?
	oo ahlay voo?
Where are you from? _____	D'où venez-vous?
	doo vuhnay voo?
How?_____	Comment?
	komohn?
How far is that? _____	C'est loin?
	seh lwahn?
How long does that take? __	Combien de temps faut-il?
	kawnbyahn duh tohn foa teel?
How long is the trip? _____	Combien de temps dure le voyage?
	kawnbyahn duh tohn dewr luh vwahyahjh?
How much?_____	Combien?
	kawnbyahn?
How much is this?_____	C'est combien?
	seh kawnbyahn?
What time is it? _____	Quelle heure est-il?
	kehl uhr eh teel?
Which? _____	Quel? Quels?/Quelle? Quelles?
	kehl?
Which glass is mine? _____	Quel est mon verre?
	kehl eh mawn vehr?

When? _____	Quand?
	kohn?
When are you leaving? ____	Quand partez-vous?
	kohn pahrtay voo?
Why? _____	Pourquoi?
	poorkwah?
Could you...me? _____	Pouvez-vous me...?
	poovay voo muh...?
Could you help me, _____ please?	Pouvez-vous m'aider s'il vous plaît?
	poovay voo mayday seel voo pleh?
Could you point that _____ out to me?	Pouvez-vous me l'indiquer?
	poovay voo muh lahndeekay?
Could you come _____ with me, please?	Pouvez-vous m'accompagner s'il vous plaît?
	poovay voo mahkawnpahnnyay seel voo pleh?
Could you... _____	Voulez-vous...?
	voolay voo...?
Could you reserve some ___ tickets for me, please?	Voulez-vous me réserver des places s'il vous plaît?
	voolay voo muh rayzehrvay day plahs seel voo pleh?
Do you know...? _____	Connaissez-vous...?
	konehssay voo...?
Do you know another _____ hotel, please?	Vous connaissez peut-être un autre hôtel?
	voo konehssay puh tehtr uhn noatr oatehl?
Do you know whether...? ___	Savez-vous si...?
	sahvay voo see...?
Do you have a...? _____	Avez-vous un...?
	ahvay voo zuhn...?
Do you have a _____ vegetarian dish, please?	Vous avez peut-être un plat sans viande?
	voo zahvay puh tehtr uhn plah sohn vyohnd?
I'd like... _____	Je voudrais...
	jhuh voodreh...
I'd like a kilo of apples, ____ please	Je voudrais un kilo de pommes
	jhuh voodreh zuhn keeloa duh pom
Can I...? _____	Puis-je...?
	pwee jhuh...?
Can I take this? _____	Puis-je prendre ceci?
	pwee jhuh prohndr suhsee?
Can I smoke here? _____	Puis-je fumer ici?
	pwee jhuh fewmay eesee?
Could I ask you _____ something?	Puis-je vous demander quelque chose?
	pwee jhuh voo duhmohnday kehlkuh shoaz?

2.3 How to reply

Yes, of course _____	Oui, bien sûr
	wee, byahn sewr
No, I'm sorry _____	Non, je suis désolé
	nawn, jhuh swee dayzolay
Yes, what can I do _____ for you?	Oui, que puis-je faire pour vous?
	wee, kuh pwee jhuh fehr poor voo?
Just a moment, please ____	Un moment s'il vous plaît
	uhn momohn seel voo pleh

No, I don't have _____ time now	Non, je n'ai pas le temps en ce moment
	nawn, jhuh nay pah luh tohn ohn suh momohn
No, that's impossible _____	Non, c'est impossible
	nawn, seh tahnposseebl
I think so _____	Je le crois bien
	jhuh luh krwah byahn
I agree _____	Je le pense aussi
	jhuh luh pohns oasee
I hope so too _____	Je l'espère aussi
	jhuh lehspehr oasee
No, not at all _____	Non, absolument pas
	nawn, ahbsolewmohn pah
No, no-one _____ __	Non, personne
	nawn, pehrson
No, nothing _____	Non, rien
	nawn, ryahn
That's (not) right _____	C'est (ce n'est pas) exact
	seht (suh neh pahz) ehgzah
I (don't) agree _____	Je suis (je ne suis pas) d'accord avec vous
	jhuh swee (jhuh nuh swee pah) dahkor ahvehk voo
All right _____	C'est bien
	seh byahn
Okay _____	D'accord
	dahkor
Perhaps _____	Peut-être
	puh tehtr
I don't know _____	Je ne sais pas
	jhuh nuh seh pah

.4 Thank you

Thank you _____	Merci/merci bien
	mehrsee/mehrsee byahn
You're welcome _____	De rien/avec plaisir
	duh ryahn/ahvehk playzeer
Thank you very much _____	Merci beaucoup
	mehrsee boakoo
Very kind of you _____	C'est aimable de votre part
	seh taymahbl duh votr pahr
I enjoyed it very much _____	C'était un réel plaisir
	sayteh tuhn rayehl playzeer
Thank you for your _____ trouble	Je vous remercie pour la peine
	jhuh voo ruhmehrsee poor lah pehn
You shouldn't have _____	Vous n'auriez pas dû
	voo noaryay pah dew
That's all right _____	Pas de problème
	pah duh problehm

Courtesies

.5 Sorry

Excuse me _____	Excusez-moi
	ehxkewzay mwah
Sorry! _____	Pardon!
	pahrdawn!
I'm sorry, I didn't know... ___	Pardon, je ne savais pas que...
	pahrdawn jhuh nuh sahveh pah kuh...
I do apologise _____	Excusez-moi
	ehxkewzay mwah
I'm sorry _____	Je suis désolé
	jhuh swee dayzolay
I didn't do it on purpose, ___ it was an accident	Je ne l'ai pas fait exprès, c'était un accident
	jhuh ne lay pah feh ehxpreh, sayteh tuhn nahxeedohn
That's all right _____	Ce n'est pas grave
	suh neh pah grahv
Never mind _____	Ça ne fait rien
	sah nuh feh ryahn
It could've happened to ___ anyone	Ça peut arriver à tout le monde
	sah puh ahreevay ah too luh mawnd

.6 What do you think?

Which do you prefer? _____	Qu'est-ce que vous préférez?
	kehs kuh voo prayfayray?
What do you think? _____	Qu'en penses-tu?
	kohn pohns tew?
Don't you like dancing? ___	Tu n'aimes pas danser?
	tew nehm pah dohnsay?
I don't mind _____	Ça m'est égal
	sah meh taygahl
Well done! _____	Très bien!
	treh byahn!
Not bad! _____	Pas mal!
	pah mahl!
Great! _____	Génial!
	jhaynyahl!
Wonderful! _____	Super!
	sewpehr!
It's really nice here! _____	C'est drôlement agréable ici!
	seh droalmohn ahgrayahbl eesee!
How nice! _____	Pas mal, chouette!
	pah mahl, shweht!
How nice for you! _____	C'est formidable!
	seh formeedahbl!
I'm (not) very happy with...	Je suis (ne suis pas) très satisfait(e) de...
	jhuh swee (nuh swee pah) treh sahteesfeh(t) duh...
I'm glad... _____	Je suis content(e) que...
	jhuh swee kawntohn(t) kuh...
I'm having a great time ___	Je m'amuse beaucoup
	jhuh mahmewz boakoo

22

I'm looking forward to it	Je m'en réjouis *jhuh mohn rayjhwee*
I hope it'll work out	J'espère que cela réussira *jhehspehr kuh suhlah rayewseerah*
That's ridiculous!	C'est nul! *seh newl!*
That's terrible!	Quelle horreur! *kehl oruhr!*
What a pity!	C'est dommage! *seh domahjh!*
That's filthy!	C'est dégoûtant! *seh daygootohn!*
What a load of rubbish!	C'est ridicule/C'est absurde! *seh reedeekewl/seh tahbsewrd!*
I don't like...	Je n'aime pas... *jhuh nehm pah...*
I'm bored to death	Je m'ennuie à mourir *jhuh mohnnwee ah mooreer*
I've had enough	J'en ai assez/ras le bol *jhohn nay ahsay/rahl bol*
This is no good	Ce n'est pas possible *suh neh pah posseebl*
I was expecting something completely different	Je m'attendais à quelque chose de très différent *jhuh mahtohndeh ah kehlkuh shoaz duh treh deefayrohn*

Conversation

Conversation

3.1 I beg your pardon?

I don't speak any/ I speak a little...	Je ne parle pas/je parle un peu... *jhuh nuh pahrl pah/jhuh pahrl uhn puh..*
I'm English	Je suis anglais/anglaise *jhuh swee zohngleh/zohnglehz*
I'm Scottish	Je suis écossais/écossaise *jhuh swee zaykosseh/zaykossehz*
I'm Irish	Je suis irlandais/irlandaise *jhuh swee zeerlohndeh/zeerlohndehz*
I'm Welsh	Je suis gallois/galloise *jhuh swee gahlwah/gahlwahz*
Do you speak English/French/German?	Parlez-vous anglais/français/allemand? *pahrlay voo ohngleh/ frohnseh/ahlmohn?*
Is there anyone who speaks...?	Y a-t-il quelqu'un qui parle...? *ee yah teel kehlkuhn kee pahrl...?*
I beg your pardon?	Que dites-vous? *kuh deet voo?*
I (don't) understand	Je (ne) comprends (pas) *jhuh (nuh) kawnprohn (pah)*
Do you understand me?	Me comprenez-vous? *me kawnpruhnay voo?*
Could you repeat that, please?	Voulez-vous répéter s'il vous plaît? *voolay voo raypaytay seel voo pleh?*
Could you speak more slowly, please?	Pouvez-vous parler plus lentement? *poovay voo pahrlay plew lohntmohn?*
What does that word mean?	Qu'est-ce que ce mot veut dire? *kehs kuh suh moa vuh deer?*
Is that similar to/the same as...?	Est-ce (environ) la même chose que...? *ehs (ohnveerawn) lah mehm shoaz kuh...?*
Could you write that down for me, please?	Pouvez-vous me l'écrire? *poovay voo muh laykreer?*
Could you spell that for me, please?	Pouvez-vous me l'épeler? *poovay voo muh laypuhlay?*

(See 1.8 Telephone alphabet)

Could you point that out in this phrase book, please?	Pouvez-vous me le montrer dans ce guide de conversation? *poovay voo muh luh mawntray dohn suh gueed duh kawnvehrsahsyawn?*
One moment, please, I have to look it up	Un moment, je dois le chercher *uhn momohn, jhuh dwah luh shehrshay*
I can't find the word/the sentence	Je ne trouve pas le mot/la phrase *jhuh nuh troov pah luh moa/lah frahz*
How do you say that in...?	Comment dites-vous cela en...? *komohn deet voo suhlah ohn...?*
How do you pronounce that?	Comment prononcez-vous cela? *komohn pronawnsay voo suhlah?*

Conversation

May I introduce myself? ___	Puis-je me présenter?
	pwee jhuh muh prayzohntay?
My name's... ___	Je m'appelle...
	jhuh mahpehl...
I'm... ___	Je suis...
	jhuh swee...
What's your name? ___	Comment vous appelez-vous?
	komohn voo zahpuhlay voo?
May I introduce...? ___	Puis-je vous présenter?
	pwee jhuh voo prayzohntay?
This is my wife/ ___ daughter/mother/ girlfriend	Voici ma femme/fille/mère/mon amie
	vwahsee mah fahm/feey/mehr/mawn nahmee
– my husband/son/ ___ father/boyfriend	Voici mon mari/fils/père/ami
	vwahsee mawn mahree/fees/pehr/ahmee
How do you do ___	Enchanté(e).
	ohnshohntay
Pleased to meet you ___	Je suis heureux(se) de faire votre connaissance
	jhuh swee zuhruh(z) duh fehr votr kohnehssohns
Where are you from? ___	D'où venez-vous?
	doo vuhnay voo?
I'm from ___ England/Scotland/ Ireland/Wales	Je viens d'Angleterre/d'Ecosse/d'Irlande/du pays de Galles
	jhuh vyahn dohngluhtehr/daykos/deerlohnd/ dew payee duh gahl
What city do you live in? ___	Vous habitez dans quelle ville?
	voo zahbeetay dohn kehl veel?
In..., It's near... ___	A...C'est à côté de...
	ah...seh tah koatay duh...
Have you been here ___ long?	Etes-vous ici depuis longtemps?
	eht voo zeesee duhpwee lawntohn?
A few days ___	Depuis quelques jours
	depwee kehlkuh jhoor
How long are you ___ staying here?	Combien de temps restez-vous ici?
	kawnbyahn duh tohn rehstay voo zeesee?
We're (probably) leaving ___ tomorrow/in two weeks	Nous partirons (probablement) demain/dans quinze jours
	noo pahrteerawn (probahbluhmohn) duhmahn/dohn kahnz jhoor
Where are you staying? ___	Où logez-vous?
	oo lojhay voo?
In a hotel/an apartment ___	Dans un hôtel/appartement
	dohn zuhn noatehl/ahpahrtuhmohn
On a camp site ___	Dans un camping
	dohn zuhn kohnpeeng
With friends/relatives ___	Chez des amis/chez de la famille
	shay day zahmee/shay duh lah fahmeey
Are you here on your ___ own/with your family?	Etes-vous ici seul/avec votre famille?
	eht voo zeesee suhl/ahvehk votr fahmeey?
I'm on my own ___	Je suis seul(e)
	jhuh swee suhl

I'm with my partner/wife/husband	Je suis avec mon ami(e)/ma femme/mon mari *jhuh swee zahvehk mawn nahmee/mah fahm/mawn mahree*
– with my family	Je suis avec ma famille *jhuh swee zahvehk mah fahmeey*
– with relatives	Je suis avec de la famille *jhuh swee zahvehk duh lah fahmeey*
– with a friend/friends	Je suis avec un ami/une amie /des amis *jhuh swee zahvehk uhn nahmee/ewn ahmee/day zahmee*
Are you married?	Etes-vous marié(e)? *eht voo mahreeay?*
Do you have a steady boyfriend/girlfriend?	As-tu un petit ami (une petite amie)? *ah tew uhn puhtee tahmee (ewn puhteet ahmee)?*
That's none of your business	Cela ne vous regarde pas *suhlah nuh voo ruhgahrd pah*
I'm married	Je suis marié(e) *jhuh swee mahreeay*
– single	Je suis célibataire *jhuh swee sayleebahtehr*
– separated	Je suis séparé(e) *jhuh swee saypahray*
– divorced	Je suis divorcé(e) *jhuh swee deevorsay*
– a widow/widower	Je suis veuf/veuve *jhuh swee vuhf/vuhv*
I live alone/with someone	J'habite tout(e) seul(e)/avec quelqu'un *jhahbeet too suhl(toot suhl)/ahvehk kehlkuhn*
Do you have any children/grandchildren?	Avez-vous des enfants/petits-enfants? *ahvay voo day zohnfohn/puhtee zohnfohn?*
How old are you?	Quel âge avez-vous? *kehl ahjh ahvay voo?*
How old is he/she?	Quel âge a-t-il/a-t-elle? *kehl ahjh ah teel/ah tehl?*
I'm...years old	J'ai...ans *jhay...ohn*
He's/she's...years old	Il/elle a...ans *eel/ehl ah...ohn*
What do you do for a living?	Quel est votre métier? *kehl eh votr maytyay?*
I work in an office	Je travaille dans un bureau *jhuh trahvahy dohn zuhn bewroa*
I'm a student/ I'm at school	Je fais des études/je vais à l'école *jhuh feh day zaytewd/jhuh veh zah laykol*
I'm unemployed	Je suis au chômage *jhuh swee zoa shoamajh*
I'm retired	Je suis retraité(e) *jhuh swee ruhtrehtay*
I'm on a disability pension	Je suis en invalidité *jhuh swee zohn nahnvahleedeetay*
I'm a housewife	Je suis femme au foyer *jhuh swee fahm oa fwahyay*
Do you like your job?	Votre travail vous plaît? *votr trahvahy voo pleh?*

3

Conversation

Most of the time _____	Ça dépend
	sah daypohn
I prefer holidays_____	J'aime mieux les vacances
	Jhehm myuh lay vahkohns

3.3 Starting/ending a conversation

Could I ask you _____ something?	Puis-je vous poser une question?
	pwee jhuh voo poazay ewn kehstyawn?
Excuse me _____	Excusez-moi
	ehxkewsay mwah
Excuse me, could you _____ help me?	Pardon, pouvez-vous m'aider?
	pahrdawn, poovay voo mayday?
Yes, what's the problem? _____	Oui, qu'est-ce qui se passe?
	wee, kehs kee suh pahss?
What can I do for you? _____	Que puis-je faire pour vous?
	kuh pwee jhuh fehr poor voo?
Sorry, I don't have time _____ now	Excusez-moi, je n'ai pas le temps maintenant
	ehxkewzay mwah, jhuh nay pah luh tohn mahntuhnohn
Do you have a light? _____	Vous avez du feu?
	voo zahvay dew fuh?
May I join you? _____	Puis-je m'asseoir à côté de vous?
	pwee jhuh mahsswahr ah koatay duh voo?
Could you take a _____ picture of me/us? Press this button.	Voulez-vous me/nous prendre en photo? Appuyez sur ce bouton.
	voolay voo muh/noo prohndr ohn foatoa? ahpweeyay sewr suh bootawn
Leave me alone _____	Laissez-moi tranquille
	laysay mwah trohnkeey
Get lost_____	Fichez le camp
	feeshay luh kohn
Go away or I'll scream_____	Si vous ne partez pas, je crie
	see voo nuh pahrtay pah, jhuh kree

3.4 Congratulations and condolences

Happy birthday/many _____ happy returns	Bon anniversaire/bonne fête
	bohn nahnneevehrsehr/bon feht
Please accept my_____ condolences	Mes condoléances
	may kawndolayohns
I'm very sorry for you _____	Cela me peine beaucoup pour vous
	suhlah muh pehn boakoo poor voo

3.5 A chat about the weather

See also 1.5 The weather

It's so hot/cold today!_____	Qu'est-ce qu'il fait chaud/froid aujourd'hui!
	kehs keel feh shoa/frwah oajhoordwee!
Nice weather, isn't it? _____	Il fait beau, n'est-ce pas?
	eel feh boa, nehs pah?
What a wind/storm! _____	Quel vent/orage!
	kehl vohn/orahjh!

All that rain/snow! _____	Quelle pluie/neige! *kehl plwee/nehjh!*
All that fog! _____	Quel brouillard! *kehl brooy-yahr!*
Has the weather been _____ like this for long here?	Fait-il ce temps-là depuis longtemps? *feh teel suh tohn lah duhpwee lawntohn?*
Is it always this hot/cold ___ here?	Fait-il toujours aussi chaud/froid ici? *feh teel toojhoor oasee shoa/frwah eesee?*
Is it always this dry/wet____ here?	Fait-il toujours aussi sec/humide ici? *feh teel toojhoor oasee sehk/ewmeed eesee?*

.6 Hobbies

Do you have any _____ hobbies?	Avez-vous des passe-temps? *ahvay voo day pahs tohn?*
I like painting/_____ reading/photography/ DIY	J'aime peindre/lire/la photo/le bricolage *jhehm pahndr/leer/lah foatoa/luh breekolahjh*
I like music _____	J'aime la musique *jhehm lah mewzeek*
I like playing the _____ guitar/piano	J'aime jouer de la guitare/du piano *jhehm jhooay duh lah gueetahr/dew pyahnoa*
I like going to the _____ movies	J'aime aller au cinéma *jhehm ahlay oa seenaymah*
I like travelling/_____ sport/fishing/walking	J'aime voyager/faire du sport/la pêche/me promener *jhehm vwahyahjhay/fehr dew spor/lah pehsh/ muh promuhnay*

.7 Being the host(ess)

See also 4 Eating out

Can I offer you a drink? ____	Puis-je vous offrir quelque chose à boire? *pwee jhuh voo zofreer kehlkuh shoaz ah bwahr?*
What would you like_____ to drink?	Que désires-tu boire? *kuh dayzeer tew bwahr?*
Something non-_____ alcoholic, please.	De préférence quelque chose sans alcool *duh prayfayrohns kehlkuh shoaz sohn zahlkol*
Would you like a _____ cigarette/cigar/to roll your own?	Voulez-vous une cigarette/un cigare/rouler une cigarette? *voolay voo zewn seegahreht/uhn seegahr/roolay ewn seegahreht?*
I don't smoke _____	Je ne fume pas *jhuh nuh fewm pah*

.8 Invitations

Are you doing anything____ tonight?	Faites-vous quelque chose ce soir? *feht voo kehlkuh shoaz suh swahr?*
Do you have any plans ____ for today/this afternoon/tonight?	Avez-vous déjà fait des projets pour aujourd'hui/cet après-midi/ce soir? *ahvay voo dayjhah feh day projheh poor oa- jhoordwee/seht ahpreh meedee/suh swahr?*
Would you like to go _____ out with me?	Aimeriez-vous sortir avec moi? *aymuhryay voo sorteer ahvehk mwah?*

Would you like to go _____ dancing with me?	Aimeriez-vous aller danser avec moi? *aymuhryay voo zahlay dohnsay ahvehk mwah?*
Would you like to have ____ lunch/dinner with me?	Aimeriez-vous déjeuner/dîner avec moi? *aymuhryay voo dayjhuhnay/deenay ahvehk mwah?*
Would you like to come____ to the beach with me?	Aimeriez-vous aller à la plage avec moi? *aymuhryay voo zahlay ah lah plahjh ahvehk mwah?*
Would you like to come____ into town with us?	Aimeriez-vous aller en ville avec nous? *aymuhryay voo zahlay ohn veel ahvehk noo?*
Would you like to come____ and see some friends with us?	Aimeriez-vous aller chez des amis avec nous? *aymuhryay voo zahlay shay day zahmee ahvehk noo?*
Shall we dance?_____	On danse? *awn dohns?*
– sit at the bar? _____	On va s'asseoir au bar? *awn vah saswahr oa bahr?*
– get something to drink? __	On va boire quelque chose? *awn vah bwahr kehlkuh shoaz?*
– go for a walk/drive?_____	On va marcher un peu/on va faire un tour en voiture? *awn vah mahrshay uhn puh/awn vah fehr uhn toor ohn vwahtewr?*
Yes, all right _____	Oui, d'accord *wee, dahkor*
Good idea _____	Bonne idée *bon eeday*
No (thank you) _____	Non (merci) *nawn (mehrsee)*
Maybe later_____	Peut-être tout à l'heure *puh tehtr too tah luhr*
I don't feel like it _____	Je n'en ai pas envie *jhuh nohn nay pah zohnvee*
I don't have time _____	Je n'ai pas le temps *jhuh nay pah luh tohn*
I already have a date _____	J'ai déjà un autre rendez-vous *jhay dayjhah uhn noatr rohnday voo*
I'm not very good at_____ dancing/volleyball/ swimming	Je ne sais pas danser/jouer au volley/nager *jhuh nuh seh pah dohnsay/jhooay oa volay/nahjhay*

3.9 Paying a compliment

You look wonderful! _____	Vous avez l'air en pleine forme! *voo zahvay lehr ohn plehn form!*
I like your car! _____	Quelle belle voiture! *kehl behl vwahtewr!*
I like your ski outfit! _____	Quelle belle combinaison de ski! *kehl behl kawnbeenehzawn duh skee!*
You're a nice boy/girl _____	Tu es un garçon/une fille sympathique *tew eh zuhn gahrsohn/ewn feey sahnpahteek*
What a sweet child! _____	Quel adorable enfant! *kehl ahdorahbl ohnfohn!*

You're a wonderful _____ dancer!	Vous dansez très bien!
	voo dohnsay treh byahn!
You're a wonderful _____ cook!	Vous faites très bien la cuisine!
	voo feht treh byahn lah kweezeen!
You're a terrific soccer _____ player!	Vous jouez très bien au football!
	voo jhooay treh byahn oa footbol!

③ .10 Chatting someone up

I like being with you _____	J'aime bien être près de toi
	jhehm byahn ehtr preh duh twah
I've missed you so much __	Tu m'as beaucoup manqué
	tew mah boakoo mohnkay
I dreamt about you _____	J'ai rêvé de toi
	jhay rehvay duh twah
I think about you all day ___	Je pense à toi toute la journée
	jhuh pohns ah twah toot lah jhoornay
You have such a sweet ___ smile	Tu souris si gentiment
	tew sooree see jhohnteemohn
You have such beautiful ___ eyes	Tu as de si jolis yeux
	tew ah duh see jhoalee zyuh
I'm in love with you _____	Je suis amoureux/se de toi
	jhuh swee zahmooruh(z) duh twah
I'm in love with you too ___	Moi aussi de toi
	mwah oasee duh twah
I love you__ _____	Je t'aime
	jhuh tehm
I love you too _____	Je t'aime aussi
	jhuh tehm oasee
I don't feel as strongly _____ about you	Je n'ai pas d'aussi forts sentiments pour toi
	jhuh nay pah doasee for sohnteemohn poor twah
I already have a _____ boyfriend/girlfriend	J'ai déjà un ami/une amie
	jhay dayjhah uhn nahmee/ewn ahmee
I'm not ready for that_____	Je n'en suis pas encore là
	jhuh nohn swee pah zohnkor lah
This is going too fast _____ for me.	Ça va un peu trop vite
	sah vah uhn puh troa veet
Take your hands off me____	Ne me touche pas
	nuh muh toosh pah
Okay, no problem _____	D'accord, pas de problème
	dahkor, pah duh problehm
Will you stay with me _____ tonight?	Tu restes avec moi cette nuit?
	tew rehst ahvehk mwah seht nwee?
I'd like to go to bed_____ with you	J'aimerais coucher avec toi
	jhehmuhreh kooshay ahvehk twah
Only if we use a_____ condom	Seulement en utilisant un préservatif
	suhlmohn ohn newteeleezohn uhn prayzehrvahteef
We have to be careful _____ about AIDS	Il faut être prudent à cause du sida
	eel foa tehtr prewdohn ah koaz dew seedah
That's what they all say____	Ils disent tous pareil
	eel deez toos pahrehy
We shouldn't take any _____ risks	Ne prenons aucun risque
	nuh pruhnawn zoakuhn reesk

Do you have a condom? ___ Tu as un préservatif?
tew ah zuhn prayzehrvahteef?

No? In that case we _____ Non? Alors je ne veux pas
won't do it *nawn? ahlor jhuh nuh vuh pah*

3 .11 Arrangements

When will I see _____ Quand est-ce que je te revois?
you again? *kohn tehs kuh jhuh tuh ruhvwah?*

Are you free over the _____ Vous êtes/tu es libre ce week-end?
weekend? *voozeht/tew eh leebr suh week-ehnd?*

What shall we arrange? ____ Que décidons-nous?
kuh dayseedawn noo?

Where shall we meet? _____ Où nous retrouvons-nous?
oo noo ruhtroovawn noo?

Will you pick me/us up? ___ Vous venez me/nous chercher?
voo vuhnay muh/noo shehrshay?

Shall I pick you up? _____ Je viens vous/te chercher?
jhuh vyahn voo/tuh shehrshay?

I have to be home by... ____ Je dois être à la maison à...heures
jhuh dwah zehtr ah lah mehzawn ah...uhr

3 .12 Saying goodbye

I don't want to see _____ Je ne veux plus vous revoir
you anymore *jhuh nuh vuh plew voo ruhvwahr*

Can I take you home? _____ Puis-je vous raccompagner à la maison?
pwee jhuh voo rahkawnpahnyay ah lah mehzawn?

Can I write/call you? _____ Puis-je vous écrire/téléphoner?
pwee jhuh voo zaykreer/taylayfonay?

Will you write/call me? ____ M'écrirez-vous/me téléphonerez-vous?
maykreeray voo/muh taylayfonuhray voo?

Can I have your _____ Puis-je avoir votre adresse/numéro de
address/phone number? téléphone?
pwee jhahvwwahr votr ahdrehs/newmayroa duh taylayfon?

Thanks for everything _____ Merci pour tout
mehrsee poor too

It was very nice _____ C'était très agréable
sayteh treh zahgrayahbl

Say hello to... _____ Présentez mes amitiés à...
prayzohntay may zahmeetyay ah...

Good luck _____ Bonne chance
bon shohns

When will you be back? ___ Quand est-ce que tu reviens?
kohn tehs kuh tew ruhvyahn?

I'll be waiting for you _____ Je t'attendrai
jhuh tahtohndray

I'd like to see you again____ J'aimerais te revoir
jhehmuhreh tuh ruhvwwahr

I hope we meet _____ J'espère que nous nous reverrons bientôt
again soon *jhehspehr kuh noo noo ruhvehrawn byahntoa*

You are welcome_____ Vous êtes le/la bienvenu(e)
voozeht luh/lah byahnvuhnew

Eating out

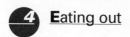

Eating out

● **In France** people usually have three meals:
1 *Le petit déjeuner* (breakfast) approx. between 7.30 and 10am. Breakfast is light and consists of *café au lait* (white coffee) or lemon tea, a croissant, or slices of baguette (French bread), with butter and jam.
2 *Le déjeuner* (lunch) approx. between midday and 2pm. Lunch always includes a hot dish and is the most important meal of the day. Offices and shops often close and lunch is taken at home, in a restaurant or canteen (in some factories and schools). It usually consists of four courses:
– starter
– main course
– cheese
– dessert
3 *Le dîner* (dinner) between 7.30 and 9pm. Dinner is a light hot meal, usually taken with the family.
At around 5pm, a special snack (*le goûter*) is served to children, usually a roll or slices of baguette and biscuits with some chocolate.

.1 On arrival

I'd like to book a table for seven o'clock, please?	Puis-je réserver une table pour sept heures? *pwee jhuh rayzehrvay ewn tahbl poor seht uhr?*
I'd like a table for two, please	Une table pour deux personnes s'il vous plaît *ewn tahbl poor duh pehrson seel voo pleh*
We've/we haven't booked	Nous (n')avons (pas) réservé *noo zahvawn/noo nahvawn pah rayzehrvay*
Is the restaurant open yet?	Le restaurant est déjà ouvert? *luh rehstoarohn eh dayjhah oovehr?*
What time does the restaurant open/close?	A quelle heure ouvre/ferme le restaurant? *ah kehl uhr oovr/fehrm luh rehstoarohn?*
Can we wait for a table?	Pouvons-nous attendre qu'une table soit libre? *poovawn noo zahtohndr kewn tahbl swah leebr?*
Do we have to wait long?	Devons-nous attendre longtemps? *devawn noo zahtohndr lawntohn?*

Vous avez réservé?	Do you have a reservation?
A quel nom?	What name, please?
Par ici, s'il vous plaît.	This way, please
Cette table est réservée.	This table is reserved
Nous aurons une table de libre dans un quart d'heure.	We'll have a table free in fifteen minutes.
Voulez-vous patienter (au bar)?	Would you like to wait (at the bar)?

Is this seat taken? _____	Est-ce que cette place est libre?
	ehs kuh seht plahs eh leebr?
Could we sit here/there? ___	Pouvons-nous nous asseoir ici/là-bas?
	poovawn noo noo zahswahr eesee/lahbah?
Can we sit by the_____	Pouvons-nous nous asseoir près de la
window?	fenêtre?
	poovawn noo noo zahswahr preh duh lah
	fuhnehtr?
Can we eat outside? _____	Pouvons-nous aussi manger dehors?
	poovawn noo zoasee mohnjhay duh-ohr?
Do you have another _____	Avez-vous encore une chaise?
chair for us?	*ahvay voo zohnkor ewn shehz?*
Do you have a highchair? __	Avez-vous une chaise haute?
	ahvay voo zewn shehz oat?
Is there a socket for _____	Y a-t-il une prise pour ce chauffe-biberon?
this bottle-warmer?	*ee ya teel ewn preez poor suh shoaf*
	beebuhrawn?
Could you warm up _____	Pouvez-vous me réchauffer ce biberon/ce
this bottle/jar for me?	petit pot?
	poovay voo muh rayshoafay suh
	beebuhrawn/suh puhtee poa?
Not too hot, please _____	Pas trop chaud s'il vous plaît
	pah troa shoa seel voo pleh
Is there somewhere I _____	Y a-t-il ici une pièce où je peux m'occuper
can change the baby's	du bébé?
nappy?	*ee ya teel eesee ewn pyehs oo jhuh puh*
	mokewpay dew baybay?
Where are the toilets? _____	Où sont les toilettes?
	oo sawn lay twahleht?

4.2 Ordering

Waiter! _____	Garçon!
	gahrsawn!
Madam! _____	Madame!
	mahdahm!
Sir!_____	Monsieur!
	muhsyuh!
We'd like something to ___	Nous aimerions manger/boire quelque
eat/a drink	chose
	noo zaymuhryawn mohnjhay/bwahr kehlkuh
	shoaz
Could I have a quick_____	Puis-je rapidement manger quelque
meal?	chose?
	pwee jhuh rahpeedmohn mohnjhay kehlkuh
	shoaz?
We don't have much _____	Nous avons peu de temps
time	*noo zavawn puh duh tohn*
We'd like to have a _____	Nous voulons d'abord boire quelque
drink first	chose
	noo voolawn dahbor bwahr kehlkuh shoaz
Could we see the_____	Pouvons-nous avoir la carte/la carte des
menu/wine list, please?	vins?
	poovawn noo zahvwahr lah kahrt/lah kahrt
	day vahn?
Do you have a menu _____	Vous avez un menu en anglais?
in English?	*voo zahvay zuhn muhnew ohn nohngleh?*

Do you have a dish _____ of the day?	Vous avez un plat du jour? *voo zahvay zuhn plah dew jhoor?*
We haven't made a _____ choice yet	Nous n'avons pas encore choisi *noo nahvawn pah zohnkor shwahzee*
What do you _____ recommend?	Qu'est-ce que vous nous conseillez? *kehs kuh voo noo kawnsayay?*
What are the specialities _____ of the region/the house?	Quelles sont les spécialités de cette région/de la maison? *kehl sawn lay spaysyahleetay duh seht rayjhyawn/duh lah mehzawn?*
I like strawberries/olives _____	J'aime les fraises/les olives *jhehm lay frehz/lay zoleev*
I don't like meat/fish/... _____	Je n'aime pas la viande/le poisson/... *jhuh nehm pah lah vyohnd/luh pwahssawn/...*
What's this? _____	Qu'est-ce que c'est? *kehs kuh seh?*
Does it have...in it? _____	Y a-t-il du/de la/des...dedans? *ee ya teel dew/duh lah/day...duhdohn?*
What does it taste like? _____	A quoi cela ressemble-t-il? *ah kwah suhlah ruhsohnbluh teel?*
Is this a hot or a _____ cold dish?	Ce plat, est-il chaud ou froid? *suh plah, eh teel shoa oo frwah?*
Is this sweet? _____	Ce plat, est-il sucré? *suh plah, eh teel sewkray?*
Is this spicy? _____	Ce plat, est-il épicé? *suh plah, eh teel aypeesay?*
Do you have anything _____ else, please?	Vous avez peut-être autre chose? *voo zahvay puh tehtr oatr shoaz?*
I'm on a salt-free diet _____	Le sel m'est interdit *luh sehl meh tahntehrdee*
I can't eat pork _____	La viande de porc m'est interdite *lah vyohnd duh por meh tahntehrdeet*
– sugar _____	Le sucre m'est interdit *luh sewkr meh tahntehrdee*
– fatty foods _____	Le gras m'est interdit *luh grah meh tahntehrdee*
– (hot) spices _____	Les épices (fortes) me sont interdites *lay zaypees (fort) muh sawn tahntehrdeet*

Vous désirez prendre un apéritif? _____	Would you like a drink first?
Vous avez déjà fait votre choix? _____	Have you decided?
Que désirez-vous boire? _____	What would you like to drink?
Bon appétit _____	Enjoy your meal
Vous désirez votre viande saignante, _____ à point ou bien cuite?	Would you like your steak rare, medium or well done?
Vous désirez un dessert/du café? _____	Would you like a dessert/coffee?

I'll have what those_____ people are having	J'aimerais la même chose que ces personnes-là *jhehmuhreh lah mehm shoaz kuh say pehrson lah*
I'd like... _____	J'aimerais... *jhehmuhreh...*
We're not having a _____ starter	Nous ne prenons pas d'entrée *noo nuh pruhnawn pah dohntray*
The child will share_____ what we're having	L'enfant partagera notre menu *lohnfohn pahrtahjhuhrah notr muhnew*
Could I have some _____ more bread, please?	Encore du pain s'il vous plaît *ohnkor dew pahn seel voo pleh*
– a bottle of water/wine____	Une autre bouteille d'eau/de vin *ewn oatr bootehy doa/duh vahn*
– another helping of... _____	Une autre portion de... *ewn oatr porsyawn duh...*
– some salt and pepper ____	Pouvez-vous apporter du sel et du poivre? *poovay voo zahportay dew sehl ay dew pwahvr?*
– a napkin _____	Pouvez-vous apporter une serviette? *poovay voo zahportay ewn sehrvyeht?*
– a spoon _____	Pouvez-vous apporter une cuillère? *poovay voo zahportay ewn kweeyehr?*
– an ashtray _____	Pouvez-vous apporter un cendrier? *poovay voo zahportay uhn sohndryay?*
– some matches_____	Pouvez-vous apporter des allumettes? *poovay voo zahportay day zahlewmeht?*
– some toothpicks_____	Pouvez-vous apporter des cure-dents? *poovay voo zahportay day kewr dohn?*
– a glass of water _____	Pouvez-vous apporter un verre d'eau? *poovay voo zahportay uhn vehr doa?*
– a straw (for the child) ____	Pouvez-vous apporter une paille (pour l'enfant)? *poovay voo zahportay ewn paheey (poor lohnfohn)?*
Enjoy your meal!_____	Bon appétit! *bohn nahpaytee!*
You too! _____	De même vous aussi *duh mehm voo zoasee*
Cheers!_____	Santé! *sohntay!*
The next round's on me ___	La prochaine tournée est pour moi *lah proshehn toornay eh poor mwah*
Could we have a doggy____ bag, please?	Pouvons-nous emporter les restes pour notre chien? *poovawn noo zohnportay lay rehst poor notr shyahn?*

.3 The bill

See also 8.2 Settling the bill

How much is this dish? ____	Quel est le prix de ce plat? *kehl eh luh pree duh suh plah?*
Could I have the bill, _____ please?	L'addition s'il vous plaît *lahdeesyawn seel voo pleh*

All together _____	Tout ensemble
	too tohnsohnbl
Everyone pays separately__	Chacun paye pour soi
	shahkuhn pehy poor swah
Could we have the menu __ again, please?	Pouvons-nous revoir la carte?
	poovawn noo ruhvwahr lah kahrt?
The...is not on the bill ____	Le...n'est pas sur l'addition
	luh...neh pah sewr lahdeesyawn

4 .4 Complaints

It's taking a very_____ long time	C'est bien long
	seh byahn lawn
We've been here an _____ hour already.	Nous sommes ici depuis une heure
	noo som zeesee duhpwee zewn uhr
This must be a mistake ____	Cela doit être une erreur
	suhlah dwah tehtr ewn ehruhr
This is not what I_____ ordered.	Ce n'est pas ce que j'ai commandé
	suh neh pah suh kuh jhay komohnday
I ordered..._____	J'ai commandé un...
	jhay komohnday uhn...
There's a dish missing_____	Il manque un plat
	eel mohnk uhn plah
This is broken/not clean ___	C'est cassé/ce n'est pas propre
	seh kahssay/suh neh pah propr
The food's cold _____	Le plat est froid
	luh plah eh frwah
– not fresh _____	Le plat n'est pas frais
	luh plah neh pah freh
– too salty/sweet/spicy_____	Le plat est trop salé/sucré/épicé
	luh plah eh troa sahlay/sewkray/aypeesay
The meat's not done_____	La viande n'est pas cuite
	lah vyohnd neh pah kweet
– overdone _____	La viande est trop cuite
	lah vyohnd eh troa kweet
– tough _____	La viande est dure
	lah vyohnd eh dewr
– off _____	La viande est avariée
	lah vyohnd eh tahvahryay
Could I have something ___ else instead of this?	Vous pouvez me donner autre chose à la place?
	voo poovay muh donay oatr shoaz ah lah plahs?
The bill/this amount is _____ not right	L'addition/cette somme n'est pas exacte
	lahdeesyawn/seht som neh pah zehgzahkt
We didn't have this_____	Ceci nous ne l'avons pas eu
	suhsee noo nuh lahvawn pah zew
There's no paper in the ____ toilet	Il n'y a plus de papier hygiénique dans les toilettes
	eel nee yah plew duh pahpyay eejhyayneek dohn lay twahleht
Do you have a _____ complaints book?	Avez-vous un registre de réclamations?
	ahvay voo zuhn ruhjheestr duh rayklahmahsyawn?
Will you call the_____ manager, please?	Voulez-vous appeler le directeur s'il vous plaît?
	voolay voo zahpuhlay luh deerehktuhr seel voo pleh?

4.5 Paying a compliment

That was a wonderful _____ meal	Nous avons très bien mangé
	noo zahvawn treh byahn mohnjhay
The food was excellent _____	Le repas était succulent
	luh ruhpah ayteh sewkewlohn
The...in particular was _____ delicious	Le...surtout était délicieux
	luh...sewrtoo ayteh dayleesyuh

4.6 The menu

apéritifs	gibier	plat principal
aperitifs	game	main course
boissons alcoolisées	hors d'oeuvres	potages
alcoholic beverages	starters	soups
boissons chaudes	légumes	service compris
hot beverages	vegetables	service included
carte des vins	plats chauds	spécialités
wine list	hot dishes	régionales
coquillages	plats froids	regional specialities
shellfish	cold dishes	viandes
desserts	plat du jour	meat dishes
sweets	dish of the day	volailles
fromages	pâtisserie	poultry
cheese	pastry	

4.7 Alphabetical list of drinks and dishes

agneau	beurre	caille
lamb	butter	quail
ail	biftec	calmar
garlic	steak	squid
amandes	bière (bière	canard
almonds	pression)	duck
ananas	beer (draught beer)	câpres
pineapple	biscuit	capers
anchois	biscuit	carpe
anchovy	boeuf	carp
anguille	beef	carte des vins
eel	boissons alcoolisées	wine list
anis	alcoholic beverages	céleri
aniseed	boissons chaudes/	celery
apéritif	froides	cerises
aperitif	hot/cold beverages	cherries
artichaut	boudin noir/blanc	champignons
artichoke	black/white pudding	mushrooms
asperge	brochet	crème chantilly
asparagus	pike	cream (whipped)
baguette	cabillaud	châtaigne
french stick	cod	chestnut
banane	café (noir/au lait)	chausson aux
banana	coffee (black/white)	pommes
		apple turnover

chou-fleur
cauliflower
choucroute
sauerkraut
chou
cabbage
choux de Bruxelles
Brussels sprouts
citron
lemon
civet de lièvre
jugged hare
clou de girofle
clove
cocktails
cocktails
cognac
brandy
concombre
cucumber
confiture
jam
consommé
broth
coquillages
shellfish
coquilles
  Saint-Jacques
scallops
cornichon
gherkin
côte/côtelette
chop
côte de boeuf
T-bone steak
côte de porc
pork chop
côtelette d'agneau
lamb chop
côtelettes dans
  l'échine
spare rib
couvert
cutlery
crabe
crab
crêpes
pancakes
crevettes grises
shrimps
crevettes roses
prawns
croissant
croissant

croque monsieur
toasted ham and
  cheese sandwich
cru
raw
crustacés
seafood
cuisses de
  grenouilles
frog's legs
cuit(à l'eau)
boiled
dattes
dates
daurade
sea bream
dessert
sweet
eau minérale
  gazeuse/non
  gazeuse
sparkling/still
  mineral water
échalote
shallot
écrevisse
crayfish
endives
chicory
entrecôte
sirloin steak
entrées
first course
épices
spices
épinards
spinach
escargots
snails
farine
flour
fenouil
fennel
fèves
broad beans
figues
figs
filet de boeuf
fillet
filet mignon
fillet steak
filet de porc
tenderloin

fines herbes
herbs
foie gras
goose liver
fraises
strawberries
framboises
raspberries
frit
fried
friture
deep-fried
fromage
cheese
fruit de la passion
passion fruit
fruits de la saison
seasonal fruits
gaufres
waffles
gigot d'agneau
leg of lamb
glace
ice cream
glaçons
ice cubes
grillé
grilled
groseilles
redcurrants
hareng
herring
haricots blancs
haricot beans
haricots verts
french beans
homard
lobster
hors d'oeuvre
starters
huîtres
oysters
jambon
  blanc/cru/fumé
ham(cooked/Parma
  style)/smoked)
jus de citron
lemon juice
jus de fruits
fruit juice
jus d'orange
orange juice

lait/demi-écrémé/ entier
milk/semi-skimmed/ full-cream

langouste
crayfish

langoustine
scampi

langue
tongue

lapin
rabbit

légumes
vegetables

lentilles
lentils

liqueur
liqueur

lotte
monkfish

loup de mer
sea bass

macaron
macaroon

maïs
sweetcorn

épis de maïs
corn (on the cob)

marron
chestnut

melon
melon

menu du jour/à la carte
menu of the day/à la carte

morilles
morels

moules
mussels

mousse au chocolat
chocolate mousse

moutarde
mustard

myrtilles
bilberries

noisette
hazelnut

noix
walnut

noix de veau
fillet of veal

oeuf à la coque/dur/au plat
egg soft/hard boiled/fried

oignon
onion

olives
olives

omelette
omelette

origan
oregano

pain au chocolat
chocolate bun

part
portion

pastis
pastis

pâtisserie
pastry

pêche
peach

petite friture
fried fish(whitebait or similar)

petits (biscuits) salés
savoury biscuits

petit pain
roll

petits pois
green peas

pigeon
pigeon

pintade
guinea fowl

plat du jour
dish of the day

plats froids/chauds
cold/hot courses

poire
pear

pois chiches
chick peas

poisson
fish

poivre
pepper

poivron
green/red pepper

pomme
apple

pommes de terre
potatoes

pommes frites
chips

poulet(blanc)
chicken(breast)

prune
plum

pruneaux
prunes

queue de boeuf
oxtail

ragoût
stew

ris de veau
sweetbread

riz
rice

rôti de boeuf (rosbif)
roast beef

rouget
red mullet

saignant
rare

salade verte
lettuce

salé/sucré
salted/sweet

sandwich
sandwich

saumon
salmon

sel
salt

service compris/non compris
service (not) included

sole
sole

soupe
soup

soupe à l'oignon
onion soup

spécialités régionales
regional specialities

sucre
sugar

thon
tuna

thym
thyme

tripes
tripe

truffes
truffles

truite
trout

truite saumonée
salmon trout

turbot
turbot

vapeur (à la)	vin blanc	vinaigre
steamed	white wine	vinegar
venaison	vin rosé	xérès
venison	rosé wine	sherry
viande hachée	vin rouge	
minced meat/mince	red wine	

Eating out

On the road

5 .1 **A**sking for directions

Excuse me, could I ask you something?	Pardon, puis-je vous demander quelque chose? *pahrdawn, pwee jhuh voo duhmohnday kehlkuh shoaz?*
I've lost my way	Je me suis égaré(e) *jhuh muh swee zaygahray*
Is there an... around here?	Connaissez-vous un...dans les environs? *konehssay voo zuhn... dohn lay zohnveerawn?*
Is this the way to...?	Est-ce la route vers...? *ehs lah root vehr...?*
Could you tell me how to get to...?	Pouvez-vous me dire comment aller à...? *poovay voo muh deer komohn tahlay ah...?*
What's the quickest way to...?	Comment puis-je arriver le plus vite possible à...? *komohn pwee jhuh ahreevay luh plew veet pohseebl ah...?*
How many kilometres is it to...?	Il y a encore combien de kilomètres jusqu'à...? *eel ee yah ohnkor kohnbyahn duh keeloamehtr jhewskah...?*
Could you point it out on the map?	Pouvez-vous me l'indiquer sur la carte? *poovay voo muh lahndeekay sewr lah kahrt?*

Je ne sais pas, je ne suis pas d'ici	I don't know, I don't know my way around here
Vous vous êtes trompé	You're going the wrong way
Vous devez retourner à...	You have to go back to...
Là-bas les panneaux vous indiqueront la route	From there on just follow the signs
Là-bas vous demanderez à nouveau votre route	When you get there, ask again

tout droit straight ahead	le carrefour the intersection	l'immeuble the building
à gauche left	la rue the street	à l'angle, au coin at the corner
à droite right	le feu (de signalisation) the traffic light	la rivière, le fleuve the river
tourner turn	le tunnel the tunnel	l'autopont the fly-over
suivre follow	le panneau `cédez la priorité' the `give way' sign	le pont the bridge
traverser cross		le passage à niveau the level crossing

| la barrière | le panneau direction... | la flèche |
| boom | the sign pointing to... | the arrow |

.2 Customs

● **Border documents** (France, Belgium, Luxembourg): valid passport, visa. For car and motorbike: valid UK driving licence and registration document, insurance document, green card, UK registration plate. Caravan: must be entered on the green card and driven with the same registration number. A warning triangle, headlamp convertors and extra headlamp bulbs must be carried. Insurance should also be upgraded.

Import and export specifications:

–Foreign currency: no restrictions

–Alcohol (aged 17 and above): 10 litres of spirits and 90 litres of wine.

–Tobacco (aged 17 and above): 800 cigarettes, 200 cigars or a kilo of tobacco. Restricted to personal consumption only.

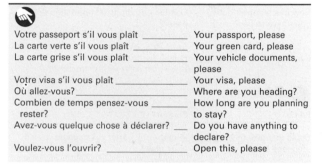

Votre passeport s'il vous plaît _____	Your passport, please
La carte verte s'il vous plaît _____	Your green card, please
La carte grise s'il vous plaît _____	Your vehicle documents, please
Votre visa s'il vous plaît _____	Your visa, please
Où allez-vous? _____	Where are you heading?
Combien de temps pensez-vous _____ rester?	How long are you planning to stay?
Avez-vous quelque chose à déclarer? ___	Do you have anything to declare?
Voulez-vous l'ouvrir? _____	Open this, please

My children are entered ___ on this passport
Mes enfants sont inscrits dans ce passeport
may zohnfohn sawn tahnskree dohn suh pahspor

I'm travelling through _____
Je suis de passage
jhuh swee duh pahsahjh

I'm going on holiday to... _
Je vais en vacances en...
jhuh veh zohn vahkohns ohn...

I'm on a business trip _____
Je suis en voyage d'affaires
jhuh swee zohn vwahyahjh dahfehr

I don't know how long _____ I'll be staying yet
Je ne sais pas encore combien de temps je reste
jhuh nuh seh pah zohnkor kawnbyahn duh tohn jhuh rehst

I'll be staying here for _____ a weekend
Je reste un week-end ici
jhuh rehst uhn weekehnd eesee

– for a few days _____
Je reste quelques jours ici
jhuh rehst kehlkuh jhoor eesee

– for a week _____
Je reste une semaine ici
jhuh rehst ewn suhmehn eesee

–for two weeks _____	Je reste quinze jours ici *jhuh rehst kahnz jhoor eesee*
I've got nothing to _____ declare	Je n'ai rien à déclarer *jhuh nay ryahn nah dayklahray*
I've got...with me _____	J'ai... avec moi *jhay... ahvehk mwah*
– ...cartons of cigarettes ___	J'ai des cartouches de cigarettes *jhay day kahrtoosh duh seegahreht*
– ...bottles of... _____	J'ai des bouteilles de... *jhay day bootehy duh...*
– some souvenirs _____	J'ai quelques souvenirs *jhay kehlkuh soovneer*
These are personal _____ effects	Ce sont des affaires personnelles *suh sawn day zahfehr pehrsonehl*
These are not new _____	Ces affaires ne sont pas neuves *say zahfehr nuh sawn pah nuhv*
Here's the receipt _____	Voici la facture *vwahsee lah fahktewr*
This is for private use _____	C'est pour usage personnel *seh poor ewzahjh pehrsonehl*
How much import duty ____ do I have to pay?	Combien de droits d'importation dois-je payer? *kawnbyahn duh drwah dahnpohrtasyawn dwah jhuh payay?*
Can I go now? _____	Puis-je partir maintenant? *pwee jhuh pahrteer mahntuhnohn?*

5 .3 Luggage

Porter! _____	Porteur! *portuhr!*
Could you take this _____ luggage to...?	Voulez-vous porter ces bagages à... s'il vous plaît? *voolay voo portay say bahgahjh ah... seel voo pleh?*
How much do I _____ owe you?	Combien vous dois-je? *kawnbyahn voo dwah jhuh?*
Where can I find a _____ luggage trolley?	Où puis-je trouver un chariot pour les bagages? *oo pwee jhuh troovay uhn shahryoa poor lay bahgahjh?*
Could you store this _____ luggage for me?	Puis-je mettre ces bagages en consigne? *pwee jhuh mehtr say bahgahjh ohn kawnseenyuh?*
Where are the luggage ____ lockers?	Où est la consigne automatique? *oo eh lah kawnseenyuh oatoamahteek?*
I can't get the locker _____ open	Je n'arrive pas à ouvrir la consigne *jhuh nahreev pah zah oovreer lah kawnseenyuh*
How much is it per item ___ per day?	Combien cela coûte-t-il par bagage par jour? *kawnbyahn suhlah koot-uh teel pahr bahgahjh pahr jhoor?*
This is not my bag/ _____ suitcase	Ce n'est pas mon sac/ma valise *suh neh pah mawn sahk/mah vahleez*

There's one item/bag/ _____ suitcase missing still	Il manque encore une chose/un sac/une valise	
	eel mohnk ohnkor ewn shoaz/uhn sahk/ewn vahleez	
My suitcase is damaged ___	Ma valise est abîmée	
	mah vahleez eh tahbeemay	

 .4 Traffic signs

accès interdit à tous les véhicules	déviation	sens unique
no entry	diversion	one-way traffic
accotement non stabilisé	fin de...	serrez à droite
soft verge	end of...	keep right
allumez vos feux	fin d'allumage des feux	sortie
switch on lights	end of need for lights	exit
autoroute	fin de chantier	sortie de camions
motorway	end of road works	factory/works exit
barrière de dégel	interdiction de dépasser	interdiction de stationner
road closed	no overtaking	no parking
bison fûté	interdiction de klaxonner	taxis
recommended route	no horns	taxi rank
brouillard fréquent	interdiction sauf riverains	travaux (sur...km)
beware fog	access only	roadworks ahead
cédez le passage	limite de vitesse	véhicules lents
give way	speed limit	slow traffic
chaussée à gravillons	passage à niveau	véhicules transportant des matières dangereuses
loose chippings	level crossing	vehicles transporting dangerous substances
chaussée déformée	passage d'animaux	verglas fréquent
uneven road surface	animals crossing	ice on road
chaussée glissante	passage pour piétons	virages sur...km
slippery road	pedestrian crossing	bends for...km
circulation alternée	péage	vitesse limite
alternate priority	toll	maximum speed
danger	poids lourds	zone bleue
danger	heavy goods vehicles	parking disc required
carrefour dangereux	rappel	zone piétonne
dangerous crossing	reminder	pedestrian zone
danger priorité à droite	remorques et semi-remorques	
priority to vehicles from right	lorries and articulated lorries	
descente dangereuse		
steep hill		

On the road

5 .5 The car

See the diagram on page 51.

● **Particular traffic regulations:**
– maximum speed for cars:
  130km/h on toll roads
  110km/h on other motorways
  90km/h outside town centres
  60km/h in town centres
– give way: all traffic from the right has the right of way, including slow
  vehicles, except for major roads.

5 .6 The petrol station

● **Petrol is more expensive** in France so it is advisable to fill up
before leaving the UK.

How many kilometres to___ the next petrol station, please?	Il y a combien de kilomètres jusqu'à la prochaine station-service? *eel ee yah kawnbyahn duh keeloamehtr jhewskah lah proshehn stasyawn sehrvees?*
I would like...litres of..., ___ please	Je voudrais ... litres *jhuh voodreh ... leetr*
– 4-star _____	Je voudrais ... litres de super *jhuh voodreh ... leetr duh sewpehr*
– leaded _____	Je voudrais ... litres d'essence ordinaire *jhuh voodreh ... leetr dehssohns ohrdeenehr*
– unleaded_____	Je voudrais ... litres d'essence sans plomb *jhuh voodreh ... leetr dehssohns sohn plawn*
– diesel _____	Je voudrais ... litres de gazoil *jhuh voodreh ... leetr duh gahzwahl*
I would like...francs_____ worth of petrol, please.	Je voudrais pour ... francs d'essence s'il vous plaît *jhuh voodreh poor ... frohn dehssohns seel voo pleh*
Fill it up, please _____	Le plein s'il vous plaît *luh plahn seel voo pleh*
Could you check...?_____	Vous voulez contrôler...? *voo voolay kawntroalay...?*
– the oil level _____	Vous voulez contrôler le niveau d'huile? *voo voolay kawntroalay luh neevoa dweel?*
– the tyre pressure _____	Vous voulez contrôler la pression des pneus? *voo voolay kawntroalay lah prehsyawn day pnuh?*
Could you change the _____ oil, please?	Vous pouvez changer l'huile? *voo poovay shohnjhay lweel?*
Could you clean the _____ windows/the windscreen, please?	Vous pouvez nettoyer les vitres/le pare-brise? *voo poovay nehtwahyay lay veetr/luh pahrbreez?*
Could you give the car_____ a wash, please?	Vous pouvez faire laver la voiture? *voo poovay fehr lahvay lah vwahtewr?*

I'm having car trouble. _____ Je suis en panne. Vous pouvez m'aider?
  Could you give me a   *jhuh swee zohn pahnn. voo poovay mayday?*
  hand?

I've run out of petrol _____ Je n'ai plus d'essence
                             jhuh neh plew dehssohns

I've locked the keys_____ J'ai laissé les clefs dans la voiture fermée
  in the car   *jhay layssay lay klay dohn lah vwahtewr*
                           fehrmay

The car/motorbike/ _____ La voiture/la moto/le vélomoteur ne
  moped won't start   démarre pas
                         lah vwahtewr/lah moatoa/luh vayloamotuhr
                         nuh daymahr pah

Could you contact the _____ Vous pouvez m'appeler l'assistance
  recovery service for me, routière?
  please?   *voo poovay mahpuhlay lahseestohns*
                            rootyehr?

Could you call a garage_____ Vous pouvez m'appeler un garage?
  for me, please?   *voo poovay mahpuhlay uhn gahrahjh?*

Could you give me _____ Puis-je aller avec vous jusqu'à ...?
  a lift to...?   *pwee jhahlay ahvehk voo jhewskah ...?*

– a garage/into town?_____ Puis-je aller avec vous jusqu'à un
                           garage/la ville?
                           pwee jhahlay ahvehk voo jhewskah uhn
                           gahrahjh/lah veel?

– a phone booth?_____ Puis-je aller avec vous jusqu'à une cabine
                      téléphonique?
                      pwee jhahlay ahvehk voo jhewskah ewn
                      kahbeen taylayfoneek?

– an emergency phone? ___ Puis-je aller avec vous jusqu'à un
                          téléphone d'urgence?
                          pwee jhalay ahvehk voo jhewskah uhn
                          taylayfon dewrjhohns?

Can we take my _____ Est-ce que vous pouvez également
  bicycle/moped?   prendre mon vélo(moteur)?
                     ehs kuh voo poovay aygahlmohn prohndr
                     mawn vayloa(motuhr)?

Could you tow me to _____ Vous pouvez me remorquer jusqu'à un
  a garage?   garage?
                         voo poovay muh ruhmorkay jhewskah uhn
                         gahrahjh?

There's probably _____ Le ... a certainement quelque chose de
  something wrong   défectueux
  with...(See page 50) *luh ... ah sehrtehnemohn kehlkuh shoaz duh*
                       dayfehktewuh

Can you fix it? _____ Vous pouvez le réparer?
                      voo poovay luh raypahray?

Could you fix my tyre? ____ Vous pouvez réparer mon pneu?
                           voo poovay raypahray mawn pnuh?

Could you change this_____ Vous pouvez changer cette roue?
  wheel?   *voo poovay shohnjhay seht roo?*

Can you fix it so it'll _____ Vous pouvez le réparer pour que je puisse
  get me to...?   rouler jusqu'à...?
                            voo poovay luh raypahray poor kuh jhuh
                            pwees roolay jhewskah...?

The parts of a car
(the diagram shows the numbered parts)

1 battery	la batterie	*lah bahtree*
2 rear light	le feu arrière	*luh fuh ahryehr*
3 rear-view mirror	le rétroviseur	*luh raytroaveezuhr*
reversing light	le phare de recul	*luh fahr duh ruhkewl*
4 aerial	l'antenne(f.)	*lohntehn*
car radio	l'autoradio(m.)	*loatoarahdyoa*
5 petrol tank	le réservoir d'essence	*luh rayzehrvwahr dehssohns*
inside mirror	le rétroviseur intérieur	*luh raytroaveezuhr ahntayryuhr*
6 sparking plugs	les bougies(f.)	*lay boojhee*
fuel filter/pump	le filtre à carburant	*luh feeltr ah kahrbewrohn*
	la pompe à carburant	*lah pawnp ah kahrbewrohn*
7 wing mirror	le rétroviseur de côté	*luh raytroaveezuhr duh koatay*
8 bumper	le pare-chocs	*luh pahr shok*
carburettor	le carburateur	*luh kahrbewrahtuhr*
crankcase	le carter	*luh kahrtehr*
cylinder	le cylindre	*luh seelahndr*
ignition	l'allumage	*l'ahlewmahjh*
warning light	la lampe témoin	*lah lohnp taymwahn*
dynamo	la dynamo	*lah deenahmoa*
accelerator	l'accélérateur	*lahksaylayrahtuhr*
handbrake	le frein à main	*luh frahn ah mahn*
valve	la soupape	*lah soopahp*
9 silencer	le silencieux	*luh seelohnsyuh*
10 boot	le coffre	*luh kofr*
11 headlight	le phare	*luh fahr*
crank shaft	le vilebrequin	*luh veelbruhkahn*
12 air filter	le filtre à air	*luh feeltr ah ehr*
fog lamp	le phare anti-brouillard	*luh fahr ohntee brooy-yahr*
13 engine block	le bloc moteur	*luh blok motuhr*
camshaft	l'arbre à cames	*lahrbr ah kahm*
oil filter/pump	le filtre à huile	*luh feeltr ah weel*
	la pompe à huile	*lah pawnp ah weel*
dipstick	la jauge du niveau d'huile	*lah jhoajh dew neevoa dweel*
pedal	la pédale	*lah paydahl*
14 door	la portière	*lah portyehr*
15 radiator	le radiateur	*luh rahdyahtuhr*
16 disc brake	le frein à disque	*luh frahn ah deesk*
spare wheel	la roue de secours	*lah roo duh suhkoor*
17 indicator	le clignotant	*luh kleenyohtohn*
18 windscreen wiper	l'essuie-glace(m.)	*lehswee glahs*
19 shock absorbers	les amortisseurs(m.)	*lay zahmorteesuhr*
sunroof	le toit ouvrant	*luh twah oovrohn*
starter motor	le démarreur	*luh daymahruhr*
20 steering column	la colonne de direction	*lah kolon duh deerehksyawn*
steering wheel	le volant	*luh volohn*

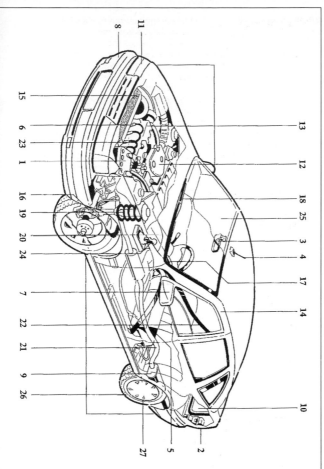

21	exhaust pipe	le tuyau d'échappement	*luh tweeyoa dayshahpmohn*
22	seat belt	la ceinture de sécurité	*lah sahntewr duh saykewreetay*
	fan	le ventilateur	*luh vohnteelahtuhr*
23	distributor cable	le câble distributeur	*luh kahbl deestreebewtuhr*
24	gear lever	le levier de vitesses	*luh luhvyay duh veetehs*
25	windscreen	le pare-brise	*luh pahrbreez*
	water pump	la pompe à eau	*lah pawnp ah oa*
26	wheel	la roue	*lah roo*
27	hubcap	l'enjoliveur	*lohnjholeevuhr*
	piston	le piston	*luh peestawn*

Which garage can _____ help me?	Quel garage pourrait m'aider?
	kehl gahrahjh pooreh mayday?
When will my car/bicycle __ be ready?	Quand est-ce que ma voiture/ma bicyclette sera prête?
	kohn tehs kuh mah vwahtewr/mah beeseekleht suhrah preht?
Can I wait for it here?_____	Je peux l'attendre ici?
	jhuh puh lahtohndr eesee?
How much will it cost? ____	Combien cela va coûter?
	kawnbyahn suhlah vah kootay?
Could you itemise_____ the bill?	Vous pouvez me détailler la note?
	voo poovay muh daytahyay lah not?
Can I have a receipt for ____ the insurance?	Puis-je avoir un reçu pour l'assurance?
	pwee jhahvwahr uhn ruhsew poor lahsewrohns?

.8 The bicycle/moped

See the diagram on page 55.

● **Cycle paths** are rare in France. Bikes can be hired at tourist centres (*vélo tout terrain* = mountain bike). Not much consideration for bikes should be expected on the roads. The maximum speed for mopeds is 45km/h both inside and outside town centres. A helmet is compulsory.

Je n'ai pas les pièces détachées pour ___ votre voiture/bicyclette	I don't have parts for your car/bicycle
Je dois aller chercher les pièces _____ détachées ailleurs	I have to get the parts from somewhere else
Je dois commander les pièces_____ détachées	I have to order the parts
Cela prendra une demi-journée _____	That'll take half a day
Cela prendra une journée_____	That'll take a day
Cela prendra quelques jours _____	That'll take a few days
Cela prendra une semaine _____	That'll take a week
Votre voiture est bonne pour la ferraille _	Your car is a write-off
Il n'y a plus rien à y faire _____	It can't be repaired
La voiture/la moto/la mobylette/la_____ bicyclette sera prête à... heures	The car/motor bike/moped/bicycle will be ready at... o'clock

I'd like to rent a... _____	J'aimerais louer un...
	jhehmuhreh looay uhn...
Do I need a (special) _____ licence for that?	Me faut-il un permis spécial?
	muh foa teel uhn pehrmee spaysyal?
I'd like to rent the...for... ___	Je voudrais louer le/la...pour
	jhuh voodreh looay luh/lah...poor
– one day _____	Je voudrais louer le/la...pour une journée
	jhuh voodreh looay luh/lah...poor ewn jhoornay
– two days _____	Je voodreh louer le/la...pour deux jours
	jhuh voodreh looay luh/lah...poor duh jhoor
How much is that per_____ day/week?	C'est combien par jour/semaine?
	seh kawnbyahn pahr jhoor/suhmehn?
How much is the _____ deposit?	De combien est la caution?
	duh kawnbyahn eh lah koasyawn?
Could I have a receipt _____ for the deposit?	Puis-je avoir un reçu pour la caution?
	pwee jhahvwahr uhn ruhsew poor lah koasyawn?
How much is the _____ surcharge per kilometre?	Quel est le supplément par kilomètre?
	kehl eh luh sewplaymohn pahr keeloamehtr?
Does that include petrol? __	Est-ce que l'essence est incluse?
	ehs kuh lehsohns eh tahnklewz?
Does that include _____ insurance?	Est-ce que l'assurance est incluse?
	ehs kuh lahsewrohns eh tahnklewz?
What time can I pick_____ the...up tomorrow?	Demain, à quelle heure puis-je venir chercher la...?
	duhmahn ah kehl uhr pwee jhuh vuhneer shehrshay lah...?
When does the...have _____ to be back?	Quand dois-je rapporter la...?
	kohn dwah jhuh rahportay lah...?
Where's the petrol tank? ___	Où est le réservoir?
	oo eh luh rayzehrvwahr?
What sort of fuel does _____ it take?	Quel carburant faut-il utiliser?
	kehl kahrbewrohn foa teel ewteeleezay?

The parts of a bicycle
(the diagram shows the numbered parts)

1 rear lamp	le feu arrière	*luh fuh ahryehr*
2 rear wheel	la roue arrière	*lah roo ahryehr*
3 (luggage) carrier	le porte-bagages	*luh port bahgahjh*
4 bicycle fork	la tête de fourche	*lah teht duh foorsh*
5 bell	la sonnette	*lah sohneht*
inner tube	la chambre à air	*lah shohnbr ah ehr*
tyre	le pneu	*luh pnuh*
6 crank	le pédalier	*luh paydahlyay*
7 gear change	le changement de vitesse	*luh shohnjhmohn duh veetehs*
wire	le fil (électrique)	*luh feel (aylehktreek)*
dynamo	la dynamo	*lah deenahmoa*
bicycle trailer	la remorque de bicyclette	*lah ruhmork duh beeseekleht*
frame	le cadre	*luh kahdr*
8 dress guard	le protège-jupe	*luh protehjh jhewp*
9 chain	la chaîne	*lah shehn*
chainguard	le carter	*luh kahrtehr*
padlock	l'antivol(m.)	*lohnteevol*
milometer	le compteur kilométrique	*luh kawntuhr keeloamaytreek*
child's seat	le siège-enfant	*luh syehjh ohnfohn*
10 headlamp	le phare	*luh fahr*
bulb	l'ampoule(f.)	*lohnpool*
11 pedal	la pédale	*lah paydahl*
12 pump	la pompe	*lah pawnp*
13 reflector	le réflecteur	*luh rayflehktuhr*
14 break blocks	les patins	*lay pahtahn*
15 brake cable	le câble de frein	*luh kahbl duh frahn*
16 wheel lock	le cadenas pour bicyclette	*lah kaduhnah poor beeseekleht*
17 carrier straps	le tendeur	*luh tohnduhr*
tachometer	le compteur de vitesse	*luh kawntuhr duh veetehs*
18 spoke	le rayon	*luh rayawn*
19 mudguard	le garde-boue	*luh gahrd boo*
20 handlebar	le guidon	*luh gueedawn*
21 chain wheel	le pignon	*luh peenyawn*
toe clip	le câle-pied	*luh kahl pyay*
22 crank axle	l'axe du pédalier(m.)	*lahx dew paydahlyay*
drum brake	le frein à tambour	*luh frahn ah tohnboor*
rim	la jante	*lah jhohnt*
23 valve	la valve	*lah vahlv*
24 valve tube	le raccord souple de la valve	*luh rahkor soopl duh lah vahlv*
25 gear cable	la chaîne du dérailleur	*lah shehn dew dayrahyuhr*
26 fork	la fourche	*lah foorsh*
27 front wheel	la roue avant	*lah roo ahvohn*
28 saddle	la selle	*lah sehl*

On the road

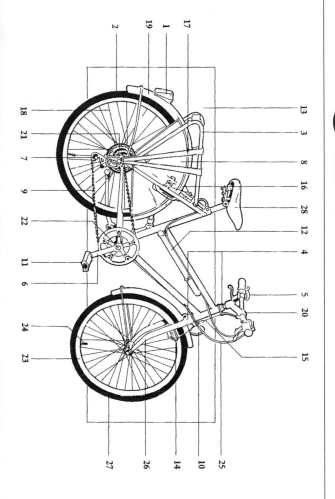

Where are you heading?	Où allez-vous?
	oo ahlay voo?
Can I come along?	Pouvez-vous m'emmener en voiture?
	poovay voo momuhnay ohn vwahtewr?
Can my boyfriend/ girlfriend come too?	Mon ami(e), peut-il/peut-elle venir avec nous?
	mawn nahmee, puh teel/puh tehl vuhneer ahvehk noo?
I'm trying to get to...	Je dois aller à...
	jhuh dwah zahlay ah...
Is that on the way to...?	C'est sur la route de...?
	seh sewr lah root duh...?
Could you drop me off...?	Vous pouvez me déposer...?
	voo poovay muh daypoazay...?
– here?	Vous pouvez me déposer ici?
	voo poovay muh daypoazay eesee?
– at the...exit?	Vous pouvez me déposer à la sortie vers...?
	voo poovay muh daypoazay ah lah sohrtee vehr...?
– in the centre?	Vous pouvez me déposer dans le centre?
	voo poovay muh daypoazay dohn luh sohntr?
– at the next roundabout?	Vous pouvez me déposer au prochain rond-point?
	voo poovay muh daypoazay oa proshahn rawnpwahn?
Could you stop here, please?	Voulez-vous arrêter ici s'il vous plaît?
	voolay voo zahrehtay eesee seel voo pleh?
I'd like to get out here	Je voudrais descendre ici
	jhuh voodreh duhsohndr eesee
Thanks for the lift	Merci pour la route
	mehrsee poor lah root

Public transport

6 **P**ublic transport

6 .1 In general

● **You can check** departure times by telephone or minitel - a computerised information system widely available in France (for example in many post offices). Tickets for buses and the *métro* (Paris, Lyon and Marseille) are cheaper when bought in a *carnet* (book of ten), available at kiosks near some bus stops, at newsagents and in *métro* stations.

Announcements

Le train de...heures, en direction de... ___ a un retard de... minutes.	The...train to...has been delayed by... minutes
Le train en direction de.../en _____ provenance de...arrive sur le quai...	The train now arriving at platform...is the...train to .../from...
Le train en direction de...va quitter le____ quai...dans quelques instants.	The train to...is about to leave from platform...
Attention éloignez-vous de la voie, un___ train rapide va passer sur la voie...	Attention please, keep your distance from the rail track, an intercity train will pass on platform...
Nous approchons la gare de... _____	We're now approaching...

Where does this train_____ go to?	Où va ce train? *oo vah suh trahn?*
Does this boat go to...? ____	Ce bateau, va-t-il à...? *suh bahtoa, vah teel ah...?*
Can I take this bus to...? ___	Puis-je prendre ce bus pour aller à...? *pwee jhuh prondr suh bews poor ahlay ah...?*
Does this train stop at...? __	Ce train s'arrête-t-il à...? *suh trahn sahreht-uh-teel ah...?*
Is this seat taken/free/ _____ reserved?	Est-ce que cette place est occupée/libre/réservée? *ehs kuh seht plahs eh tokewpay/leebr/rayzehrvay?*
I've booked... _____	J'ai réservé... *jhay rayzehrvay...*
Could you tell me _____ where I have to get off for... ?	Voulez-vous me dire où descendre pour...? *voolay voo muh deer oo duhsohndr poor...?*
Could you let me_____ know when we get to...?	Voulez-me prévenir lorsque nous serons à...? *voolay voo muh prayvuhneer lorskuh noo suhrawn zah...?*
Could you stop at the_____ next stop, please?	Voulez-vous vous arrêter au prochain arrêt s'il vous plaît? *voolay voo voo zahrehtay oa proshahn nahreht seel voo pleh?*

Where are we now? _____	Où sommes-nous ici?	
	oo som noo zeesee?	
Do I have to get off_____ here?	Dois-je descendre ici?	
	dwah jhuh duhsohndr eesee?	
Have we already _____ passed...?	Avons-nous déjà dépassé...?	
	ahvawn noo dayjhah daypahsay...?	
How long have I been _____ asleep?	Combien de temps ai-je dormi?	
	kawnbyahn duh tohn ay jhuh dormee?	
How long does... _____ stop here?	Combien de temps...reste ici?	
	kawnbyahn duh tohn...rehst eesee?	
Can I come back on the____ same ticket?	Puis-je revenir avec ce billet?	
	pwee jhuh ruhvuhneer ahvehk suh beeyeh?	
Can I change on this_____ ticket?	Puis-je prendre une correspondance avec ce billet?	
	pwee jhuh prondr ewn korehspawndohns ahvehk suh beeyeh?	
How long is this ticket _____ valid for?	Combien de temps ce billet reste-t-il valable?	
	kawnbyahn duh tohn suh beeyeh rehst-uh-teel vahlahbl?	
How much is the _____ supplement for the TGV (high speed train)?	Combien coûte le supplément pour le TGV?	
	kawnbyahn koot luh sewplaymohn poor luh tayjhayvay?	

.2 Questions to passengers

Ticket types

Première classe ou deuxième classe? ___	First or second class?
Aller simple ou retour?_____	Single or return?
Fumeurs ou non fumeurs?_____	Smoking or non-smoking?
Côté fenêtre ou côté couloir? _____	Window or aisle?
A l'avant ou à l'arrière?_____	Front or back?
Place assise ou couchette? _____	Seat or couchette?
Au-dessus, au milieu ou au-dessous? ___	Top, middle or bottom?
Classe touriste ou classe affaires?_____	Tourist class or business class?
Une cabine ou un fauteuil? _____	Cabin or seat?
Une personne ou deux personnes? _____	Single or double?
Vous êtes combien de personnes à_____ voyager?	How many are travelling?

Destination

Où allez-vous?_____	Where are you travelling?
Quand partez-vous?_____	When are you leaving?
Votre...part à... _____	Your...leaves at...
Vous devez prendre une_____ correspondance	You have to change trains
Vous devez descendre à... _____	You have to get off at...

Vous devez passer par...	You have to travel via...
L'aller est le...	The outward journey is on...
Le retour est le...	The return journey is on...
Vous devez être à bord au plus tard à...	You have to be on board by...

On board

Votre billet s'il vous plaît	Your ticket, please
Votre réservation s'il vous plaît	Your reservation, please
Votre passeport s'il vous plaît	Your passport, please
Vous n'êtes pas à la bonne place	You're in the wrong seat
Vous êtes dans le mauvais...	You're on/in the wrong...
Cette place est réservée	This seat is reserved
Vous devez payer un supplément	You'll have to pay a supplement
Le...a un retard de...minutes	The...has been delayed by...minutes

6 .3 Tickets

Where can I...?	Où puis-je...?
	oo pwee jhuh...?
– buy a ticket?	Où puis-je acheter un billet?
	oo pwee jhahshtay uhn beeyeh?
– make a reservation?	Où puis-je réserver une place?
	oo pwee jhuh rayzehrvay ewn plahs?
– book a flight?	Où puis-je réserver un vol?
	oo pwee jhuh rayzehrvay uhn vol?
Could I have a...to..., please?	Puis-je avoir...en direction de...?
	pwee jhahvwahr...ohn deerehksyawn duh...?
– a single	Puis-je avoir un aller simple?
	pwee jhahvwahr uhn nahlay sahnpl?
– a return	Puis-je avoir un aller-retour?
	pwee jhahvwahr uhn nahlay ruhtoor?
first class	première classe
	pruhmyehr klahs
second class	deuxième classe
	duhzyehm klahs
tourist class	classe touriste
	klahs tooreest
business class	classe affaires
	klahs ahfehr
I'd like to book a seat/couchette/cabin	Je voudrais réserver une place assise/couchette/cabine
	jhuh voodreh rayzehrvay ewn plahs ahseez/koosheht/kahbeen
I'd like to book a berth in the sleeping car	Je voudrais réserver une place dans le wagon-lit
	jhuh voodreh rayzehrvay ewn plahs dohn luh vahgawnlee

top/middle/bottom _____	au-dessus/au milieu/au-dessous
	oaduhsew/ oa meelyuh/ oa duhsoo
smoking/no smoking _____	fumeurs/non fumeurs
	fewmuhr/ nawn fewmuhr
by the window _____	à côté de la fenêtre
	ah koatay duh lah fenehtr
single/double _____	une personne/deux personnes
	ewn pehrson/duh pehrson
at the front/back_____	à l'avant/à l'arrière
	ah lahvohn/ah lahryehr
There are...of us_____	Nous sommes...personnes
	noo som...pehrson
a car _____	une voiture
	ewn vvwahtewr
a caravan _____	une caravane
	ewn kahrahvahnn
...bicycles _____	...bicyclettes
	...beeseekleht
Do you also have...? _____	Avez-vous aussi...?
	ahvay voo zoasee...?
– season tickets? _____	Avez-vous aussi une carte d'abonnement?
	ahvay voo zoasee ewn kahrt dahbonmohn?
– weekly tickets? _____	Avez-vous aussi une carte hebdomadaire?
	ahvay voo zoasee ewn kahrt ehbdomahdehr?
– monthly season _____ tickets?	Avez-vous aussi une carte mensuelle?
	ahvay voo zoasee ewn kahrt mohnsewehl?

6 .4 Information

Where's? _____	Où se trouve...?
	oo suh troov...?
Where's the information ___ desk?	Où se trouve le bureau de renseignements?
	oo suh troov luh bewroa duh rohnsehnyuhmohn?
Where can I find a_____ timetable?	Où se trouvent les horaires des départs/des arrivées?
	oo se troov lay zorehr day daypahr/day zahreevay?
Where's the...desk? _____	Où se trouve la réception de...?
	oo se troov lah raysehpsyawn duh...?
Do you have a city map____ with the bus/the underground routes on it?	Avez-vous un plan du réseau des bus/du métro?
	ahvay voo zuhn plohn dew rayzoa day bews/dew maytroa?
Do you have a _____ timetable?	Avez-vous un horaire des arrivées et des départs?
	ahvay voo zuhn norehr day zahreevay ay day daypahr?
I'd like to confirm/_____ cancel/change my booking for...	Je veux confirmer/annuler/changer ma réservation pour...
	jhuh vuh kawnfeermay/ahnewlay/shohnjhay mah rayzehrvahsyawn poor...
Will I get my money_____ back?	Mon argent me sera rendu?
	mawn nahrjhohn muh suhrah rohndew?

I want to go to... _____	Je dois aller à...Comment puis-je y aller
How do I get there?	(le plus vite possible)?
(What's the quickest way	*jhuh dwah zahlay ah...komohn pwee jhee*
there?)	*ahlay (luh plew veet poseebl?)*
How much is a _____	Combien coûte un aller simple/un aller-
single/return to...?	retour pour...?
	kawnbyahn koot uhn nahlay sahnpl/uhn
	nahlay retoor poor...?
Do I have to pay a _____	Dois-je payer un supplément?
supplement?	*dwah jheuh payay uhn sewplaymohn?*
Can I interrupt my _____	Puis-je interrompre mon voyage avec ce
journey with this ticket?	billet?
	pwee jhahntayrawnpr mawn vwahyahjh
	ahvehk suh beeyeh?
How much luggage _____	J'ai droit à combien de bagages?
am I allowed?	*jhay drwah ah kawnbyahn duh bahgahjh?*
Does this...travel direct? ___	Ce...est direct?
	suh...eh deerehkt?
Do I have to change? _____	Dois-je changer? Où?
Where?	*dwah jhuh shohnjhay? oo?*
Will this plane make any ___	L'avion fait escale?
stopovers?	*lahvyawn feh tehskahl?*
Does the boat call in at ____	Est-ce que le bateau fait escale dans un
any ports on the way?	port pendant son trajet?
	ehs kuh luh bahtoa feh tehskahl dohn zuhn
	por pohndohn sawn trahjheh?
Does the train/ _____	Est-ce que le train/le bus s'arrête à...?
bus stop at...?	*ehs kuh luh trahn/luh bews sahreht ah...?*
Where should I get off? ____	Où dois-je descendre?
	oo dwah jhuh duhsohndr?
Is there a connection _____	Y a-t-il une correspondance pour...?
to...?	*ee yah teel ewn korehspawndohns poor...?*
How long do I have to ____	Combien de temps dois-je attendre?
wait?	*kawnbyahn duh tohn dwah jhahtohndr?*
When does...leave? _____	Quand part...?
	kohn pahr...?
What time does the _____	A quelle heure part le
first/next/last...leave?	premier/prochain/dernier...?
	ah kehl uhr pahr luh
	pruhmyay/proshahn/dehrnyay...?
How long does...take? ____	Combien de temps met le...?
	kawnbyahn duh tohn meh luh...?
What time does...arrive ____	A quelle heure arrive...à...?
in...?	*ah kehl uhr ahreev...ah...?*
Where does the...to... _____	D'où part le...pour...?
leave from?	*doo pahr luh...poor...?*
Is this...to...? _____	Est-ce le...pour...?
	ehs luh...poor...?

.5 **A**eroplanes

● **At arrival** at a French airport (*aéroport*), you will find the following signs:

arrivée	départ
arrivals	departures

.6 **T**rains

● **The rail network** is extensive. *La Société Nationale des Chemins de Fer Français (SNCF)* is responsible for the national rail traffic. Besides the normal train, there is also *le Train à Grande Vitesse (TGV)* for which you will have to pay a supplement. Reservations before departure are cheaper. The *TGV* operates between the larger cities: Paris, Lyon, Marseille and Nice. A train ticket has to be stamped (*composté*) before departure.

.7 **T**axis

● **In nearly all** large cities, there are plenty of taxis. French taxis have no fixed colour. Virtually all taxis have a meter. In the smaller towns, it is usual to agree a fixed price in advance. A supplement is usual for luggage, a journey at night, on a Sunday or Bank holiday, or to an airport. It is advisable in large cities such as Paris and Lyon to check that the meter has been returned to zero at the start of the journey.

Public transport

libre	occupé	station de taxis
for hire	booked	taxi rank

Taxi! _____	Taxi!
	tahksee!
Could you get me a taxi, ___ please?	Pouvez-vous m'appeler un taxi?
	poovay voo mahpuhlay uhn tahksee?
Where can I find a taxi___ around here?	Où puis-je prendre un taxi par ici?
	oo pwee jhuh prohndr uhn tahksee pahr eesee?
Could you take me to..., ___ please?	Conduisez-moi à...s'il vous plaît.
	kawndweezay mwah ah...seel voo pleh
– this address _____	Conduisez-moi à cette adresse.
	kawndweezay mwah ah seht ahdrehs
– the...hotel _____	Conduisez-moi à l'hôtel...
	kawndweezay mwah ah loatehl...
– the town/city centre_____	Conduisez-moi dans le centre.
	kawndweezay mwah dohn luh sohntr
– the station _____	Conduisez-moi à la gare.
	kawndweezay mwah ah lah gahr
– the airport _____	Conduisez-moi à l'aéroport.
	kawndweezay mwah ah layroapor.
How much is the _____ trip to...?	Combien coûte un trajet jusqu'à...?
	kawnbyahn koot uhn trahjheh jhewskah...?

How far is it to...? _____	C'est combien de kilomètres jusqu'à...?
	seh kawnbyahn duh keeloamehtr
	jhewskah...?
Could you turn on the _____ meter, please?	Voulez-vous mettre le compteur en marche s'il vous plaît?
	voolay voo mehtr luh kawntuhr ohn mahrsh seel voo pleh?
I'm in a hurry _____	Je suis pressé.
	jhuh swee prehssay
Could you speed up/slow __ down a little?	Vous pouvez rouler plus vite/plus lentement?
	voo poovay roolay plew veet/plew lohntmohn?
Could you take a _____ different route?	Vous pouvez prendre une autre route?
	voo poovay prohndr ewn oatr root?
I'd like to get out here,_____ please	Je voudrais descendre ici
	jhuh voodreh duhsohndr eesee
You have to go...here _____	Là vous allez...
	lah voo zahlay...
You have to go straight ____ on here	Là vous allez tout droit
	lah voo zahlay too drwah
You have to turn left_____ here	Là vous allez à gauche
	lah voo zahlay zah goash
You have to turn right _____ here	Là vous allez à droite
	lah voo zahlay zah drwaht
This is it _____	C'est ici
	seht eesee
Could you wait a minute___ for me, please?	Vous pouvez m'attendre un instant?
	voo poovay mahtohndr uhn nahnstohn?

Overnight accommodation

Overnight accommodation

.1 General

● **There is great variety** of overnight accommodation in France.
Hôtels: stars indicate the degree of comfort; from five stars, the most luxurious, to one star, very simple. Beside the star one often finds the letters *NN-Nouvelles Normes* (new classifications). This means that the star-classification is up-to-date. Most hotels offer *pension complète* (full board) or *demi-pension* (half board).
Auberges et Relais de campagne: luxurious; splendid view and lots of rest are guaranteed.
Châteaux, Hôtels de France and Vieilles Demeures: a very expensive tourist residence, always within a castle, country manor or an historic building.
Logis de France: an organisation with many hotels with one or two stars, mostly outside the town centre. The hotel can be recognised by the yellow signboards with a green fireplace and the words: *logis de France*.
Motels: especially along the motorway, comparable to UK motels.
Auberges de jeunesse (youth hostel): the number of nights is restricted to between three and seven.
Camping: free camping is allowed, except for forest areas with the sign *attention au feu* (fire hazard). Not all camping sites are guarded.
Refuges et gîtes d'étape (mountain huts): in the Alps and Pyrenees. These huts are owned by the *Club Alpin Français* and are inexpensive.

Combien de temps voulez-vous rester?	How long will you be staying?
Voulez-vous remplir ce questionnaire s'il vous plaît?	Fill out this form, please
Puis-je avoir votre passeport?	Could I see your passport?
Vous devez payer un acompte	I'll need a deposit
Vous devez payer à l'avance	You'll have to pay in advance

My name's...I've made a reservation over the phone/by mail	Mon nom est...J'ai réservé une place par téléphone/par lettre *mawn nawn eh...jhay rayzehrvay ewn plahs pahr taylayfon/pahr lehtr*
How much is it per night/week/ month?	Quel est le prix pour une nuit/une semaine/un mois? *kehl eh luh pree poor ewn nwee/ewn suhmehn/uhn mwah?*
We'll be staying at least...nights/weeks	Nous restons au moins...nuits/semaines. *noo rehstawn zoa mwhan...nwee/suhmehn*
We don't know yet	Nous ne le savons pas encore exactement. *noo nuh luh sahvawn pah zohnkor ehgzahktmohn*
Do you allow pets (cats/dogs)?	Est-ce que les animaux domestiques(chiens/chats) sont admis? *ehs kuh lay zahneemoa domehsteek(shyahn/shah) sawn tahdmee?*

66

What time does the _____ gate/door open/close?	A quelle heure on ouvre/ferme le portail/la porte?
	ah keh uhr awn noovr/fehrm luh portahy/lah port?
Could you get me _____ a taxi, please?	Vous voulez m'appeler un taxi?
	voo voolay mahplay uhn tahksee?
Is there any mail _____ for me?	Y a-t-il du courrier pour moi?
	ee yah teel dew kooryay poor mwah?

.2 Camping

See the diagram on page 69

Vous pouvez vous-même choisir _____ votre emplacement.	You can pick your own site
Votre emplacement vous sera attribué. __	You'll be allocated a site
Voici votre numéro d'emplacement. _____	This is your site number
Vous devez coller ceci sur votre_____ voiture.	Stick this on your car, please
Ne perdez surtout pas cette carte. _____	Please don't lose this card

Where's the manager? _____	Où est le gardien?
	oo eh luh gahrdyahn?
Are we allowed to_____ camp here?	Pouvons-nous camper ici?
	poovawn noo kohnpay eesee?
There are...of us and _____ ...tents	Nous sommes...personnes et nous avons...tentes.
	noo som...pehrson ay nooz ahvawn...tohnt
Can we pick our_____ own place?	Pouvons-nous choisir nous-mêmes un emplacement?
	poovawn noo shwahzeer noo mehm uhn nohnplahsmohn?
Do you have a quiet _____ spot for us?	Avez-vous un endroit calme pour nous?
	ahvay voo zuhn nohndrwah kahlm poor noo?
Do you have any other _____ pitches available?	Vous n'avez pas d'autre emplacement libre?
	voo nahvay pah doatr ohnplahsmohn leebr?
It's too windy/sunny/ _____ shady here.	Ici il y a trop de vent/soleil/ombre.
	eesee eel ee yah troa duh vohn/sohlehy/awnbr
It's too crowded here _____	Il y a trop de monde ici.
	eel ee yah troa duh mawnd eesee
The ground's too _____ hard/uneven	Le sol est trop dur/irrégulier.
	luh sohl eh troa dewr/eeraygewlyay
Do you have a level _____ spot for the camper/ caravan/folding caravan?	Avez-vous un endroit plat pour le camping-car/la caravane/la caravane pliante?
	ahvay voo zuhn nohndrwah plah poor luh kohnpeeng kahr/lah kahrahvahnn/lah kahrahvahnn plyohnt?
Could we have _____ adjoining pitches?	Pouvons-nous être l'un à côté de l'autre?
	poovawn noo zehtr luhn nah koatay duh loatr?

Camping equipment
(the diagram shows the numbered parts)

luggage space	l'espace (f.) bagages	*lehspahs bahgajh*
can opener	l'ouvre-boîte (m.)	*loovr bwaht*
butane gas bottle	la bouteille de butane	*lah bootehy duh bewtahnn*
1 pannier	la sacoche de vélo	*lah sahkosh duh vayloa*
2 gas cooker	le réchaud à gaz	*luh rayshoa ah gahz*
3 groundsheet	le tapis de sol	*luh tahpee duh sol*
mallet	le marteau	*luh mahrtoa*
hammock	le hamac	*luh ahmahk*
4 jerry can	le bidon d'essence	*luh beedawn dehssohns*
campfire	le feu de camp	*luh fuh duh kohn*
5 folding chair	la chaise pliante	*lah shehz plyohnt*
6 insulated picnic box	la glacière	*lah glahsyehr*
ice pack	le bac à glaçons	*luh bah kah glasawn*
compass	la boussole	*lah boosol*
wick	la mèche	*lah mehsh*
corkscrew	le tire-bouchon	*luh teer booshawn*
7 airbed	le matelas pneumatique	*luh mahtuhlah pnuhmahteek*
8 airbed plug	le bouchon du matelas pneumatique	*luh booshawn dew mahtuhlah pnemahteek*
pump	la pompe à air	*lah pawnp ah ehr*
9 awning	l'auvent (m.)	*loavohn*
10 karimat	la natte	*lah naht*
11 pan	la casserole	*lah kahsrol*
12 pan handle	la poignée de casserole	*lah pwahnnyay duh kahsrol*
primus stove	le réchaud à pétrole	*luh rayshoa ah paytrol*
zip	la fermeture éclair	*lah fehrmuhtewr ayklehr*
13 backpack	le sac à dos	*luh sahk ah doa*
14 guy rope	la corde	*lah kord*
sleeping bag	le sac de couchage	*luh sahk duh kooshajh*
15 storm lantern	la lanterne-tempête	*lah lohntehrn-tohnpeht*
camp bed	le lit de camp	*luh lee duh kohn*
table	la table	*lah tahbl*
16 tent	la tente	*lah tohnt*
17 tent peg	le piquet	*luh peekeh*
18 tent pole	le mât	*luh mah*
vacuum flask	la bouteille thermos	*lah bootehy tehrmos*
19 water bottle	la gourde	*lah goord*
clothes peg	la pince à linge	*lah pahns ah lahnjh*
windbreak	le pare-vent	*luh pahrvohn*
20 torch	la torche électrique	*lah torsh aylehktreek*
pocket knife	le canif	*luh kahneef*

Overnight accommodation

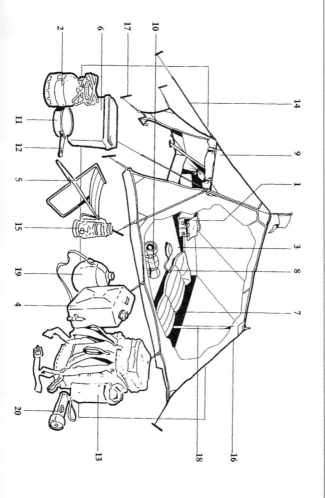

Can we park the car _____ next to the tent?	La voiture, peut-elle être garée à côté de la tente?
	lah vwahtewr, puh tehl ehtr gahray ah koatay duh lah tohnt?
How much is it per _____ person/tent/caravan/car?	Quel est le prix par personne/tente/caravane/voiture?
	kehl eh luh pree pahr pehrson/tohnt/kahrahvahnn/vwahtewr?
Are there any...? _____	Y a-t-il...?
	ee yah teel...?
– any hot showers? _____	Y a-t-il des douches avec eau chaude?
	ee yah teel day doosh ahvehk oa shoad?
– washing machines? _____	Y a-t-il des machines à laver?
	ee yah teel day mahsheen ah lahvay?
Is there a...on the site? ____	Y a-t-il un...sur le terrain?
	ee ayh teel uhn...sewr luh tehrahn?
Is there a children's _____ play area on the site?	Y a-t-il un terrain de jeux pour les enfants?
	ee yah teel uhn tehrahn duh jhuh poor lay zohnfohn?
Are there covered _____ cooking facilities on the site?	Y a-t-il un endroit couvert pour cuisiner?
	ee yah teel uhn nohndrwa koovehr poor kweezeenay?
Can I rent a safe here? ____	Puis-je louer un coffre-fort ici?
	pwee jhuh looay uhn kofr for eesee?
Are we allowed to _____ barbecue here?	Pouvons-nous faire un barbecue?
	poovawn noo fehr uhn bahrbuhkew?
Are there any power_____ points?	Y a-t-il des prises électriques?
	ee yah teel day preez aylehktreek?
Is there drinking water? ____	Y a-t-il de l'eau potable?
	ee yah teel duh loa potabl?
When's the rubbish _____ collected?	Quand vide-t-on les poubelles?
	kohn veed-uh-tawn lay poobehl?
Do you sell gas bottles ____ (butane gas/propane gas)?	Vendez-vous des bouteilles de gaz (butane/propane)?
	vohnday voo day bootehuhy duh gahz (bewtahnn/propahnn)?

7 .3 Hotel/B&B/apartment/holiday house

Do you have a _____ single/double room available?	Avez-vous une chambre libre pour une personne/deux personnes?
	ahvay voo zewn shohnbr leebr poor ewn pehrson/duh pehrson?
per person/per room _____	par personne/par chambre
	pahr pehrson/pahr shohnbr
Does that include _____ breakfast/lunch/dinner?	Est-ce que le petit déjeuner/le déjeuner/le dîner est compris?
	ehs kuh luh puhtee dayjhuhnay/luh dayjhuhnay/luh deenay eh kawnpree?
Could we have two _____ adjoining rooms?	Pouvons-nous avoir deux chambres contiguës?
	poovawn noo zahvwahr duh shohnbr kawnteegew?
with/without _____ toilet/bath/shower	avec/sans toilettes/salle de bains/douche
	ahvehk/sohn twahleht/sahl duh bahn/doosh

(not) facing the street_____	(pas) du côté rue
	(pah) dew koatay rew
with/without a view _____ of the sea	avec/sans vue sur la mer
	ahvehk/sohn vew sewr lah mehr
Is there...in the hotel?_____	Y a-t-il...dans l'hôtel?
	ee yah teel...dohn loatehl?
Is there a lift in the hotel?	Y a-t-il un ascenseur dans l'hôtel?
	ee yah teel uhn nahsohnsuhr dohn loatehl?
Do you have room service?	Y a-t-il un service de chambre dans l'hôtel?
	ee yah teel uhn sehrvees duh shohnbr dohn loatehl?

Les toilettes et la douche sont au _____ même étage/dans votre chambre	You can find the toilet and shower on the same floor/en suite
De ce côté, s'il vous plaît _____	This way, please
Votre chambre est au...étage, c'est le____ numéro...	Your room is on the... floor, number...

Could I see the room? _____	Puis-je voir la chambre?
	pwee jhuh vwhar lah shohnbr?
I'll take this room_____	Je prends cette chambre.
	jhuh prohn seht shohnbr
We don't like this one _____	Celle-ci ne nous plaît pas.
	sehl see nuh noo pleh pah
Do you have a larger/_____ less expensive room?	Avez-vous une chambre plus grande/moins chère?
	avay voo zewn shohnbr plew grohnd/mwahn shehr?
Could you put in a cot? ____	Pouvez-vous y ajouter un lit d'enfant?
	poovay voo zee ahjhootay uhn lee dohnfohn?
What time's breakfast? ____	A quelle heure est le petit déjeuner?
	ah kehl uhr eh luh puhtee dayjhuhnay?
Where's the dining room?	Où est la salle à manger?
	oo eh lah sahl ah mohnjhay?
Can I have breakfast_____ in my room?	Puis-je prendre le petit déjeuner dans la chambre?
	pwee jhuh prohndr luh puhtee dayjhuhnay dohn lah shohnbr?
Where's the emergency____ exit/fire escape?	Où est la sortie de secours/l'escalier de secours?
	oo eh lah sortee duh suhkoor/lehskahlyay duh suhkoor?
Where can I park my _____ car (safely)?	Où puis-je garer ma voiture (en sécurité)?
	oo pwee jhuh gahray mah vwahtewr (ohn saykewreetay)?
The key to room..., _____ please	La clef de la chambre..., s'il vous plaît.
	lah klay duh lah shohnbr...,seel voo pleh
Could you put this in _____ the safe, please?	Puis-je mettre ceci dans votre coffre-fort?
	pwee jhuh mehtr suhsee dohn votr kofr for?

7

Overnight accommodation

Could you wake me _____ at...tomorrow?	Demain voulez-vous me réveiller à...heures? *duhmahn voolay voo muh rayvehyay ah...uhr?*
Could you find a _____ babysitter for me?	Pouvez-vous m'aider à trouver une baby-sitter? *poovay voo mayday ah troovay ewn behbee seetehr?*
Could I have an extra _____ blanket?	Puis-je avoir une couverture supplémentaire? *pwee jhahvwahr ewn koovehrtewr sewplaymohntehr?*
What days do the _____ cleaners come in?	Quels jours fait-on le ménage? *kehl jhoor feh tawn luh maynahjh?*
When are the sheets/ _____ towels/tea towels changed?	Quand change-t-on les draps/les serviettes-éponge/les torchons? *kohn shohnjh tawn lay drah/lay sehrvyeht aypawnjh/lay tohrshawn?*

⑦ .4 Complaints

We can't sleep for _____ the noise	Nous ne pouvons pas dormir à cause du bruit *noo nuh poovawn pah dormeer ah koaz dew brwee*
Could you turn the _____ radio down, please?	Est-ce que vous pouvez baisser un peu la radio? *ehs kuh voo poovay behssay uhn puh lah rahdyoa?*
We're out of toilet paper ___	Il n'y a plus de papier hygiénique *eel nee yah plew duh pahpyay eejhyayneek*
There aren't any.../there's ___ not enough...	Il n'y a pas de/pas assez de... *eel nee yah pah duh/pah zahssay duh...*
The bed linen's dirty _____	La literie est sale *lah leetree eh sahl*
The room hasn't been _____ cleaned	La chambre n'a pas été nettoyée *lah shohnbr nah pah zayatay nehtwahyay*
The kitchen is not clean _____	La cuisine n'est pas propre *lah kweezeen neh pah propr*
The kitchen utensils are _____ dirty	Les ustensiles de cuisine sont sales *lay zewstohnseel duh kweezeen sawn sahl*
The heater's not _____ working	Le chauffage ne marche pas *luh shoafajh nuh marsh pah*
There's no (hot) _____ water/electricity	Il n'y a pas d'eau(chaude)/d'électricité *eel nee yah pah doa(shoad)/daylehktreeseetay*
...is broken _____	...est cassé *...eh kahssay*
Could you have that _____ seen to?	Vous pouvez le faire réparer? *voo poovay luh fehr raypahray?*
Could I have another _____ room/site?	Puis-je avoir une autre chambre/un autre emplacement pour la tente? *pwee jhuh ahvwahr ewn oatr shohnbr/uhn noatr ohnplasmohn poor lah tohnt?*
The bed creaks terribly _____	Le lit grince énormément *luh lee grahns aynormaymohn*
The bed sags _____	Le lit s'affaisse *luh lee sahfehs*

There are bugs/insects_____ in our room	Nous sommes incommodés par des bestioles/insectes *noo som zahnkomoday pahr day behstyol/day zahnsehkt*
This place is full_____ of mosquitos	C'est plein de moustiques ici *seh plahn duh moosteek eesee*
– cockroaches_____	C'est plein de cafards *seh plahn duh kahfahr*

 **.5 D**eparture

See also 8.2 Settling the bill

I'm leaving tomorrow. _____ Could I settle my bill, please?	Je pars demain. Puis-je payer maintenant? *jhuh pahr duhmahn. pwee jhuh payay mahntuhnohn?*
What time should we_____ vacate?	A quelle heure devons-nous quitter la chambre? *ah kehl uhr duhvawn noo keetay lah shohnbr?*
Could I have my passport__ back, please?	Pouvez-vous me rendre mon passeport? *poovay voo muh rohndr mawn pahspor?*
We're in a terrible hurry ___	Nous sommes très pressés *noo som treh prehssay*
Could you forward _____ my mail to this address?	Pouvez-vous faire suivre mon courrier à cette adresse? *poovay voo fehr sweevr mawn kooryay ah seht ahdrehs?*
Could we leave our_____ luggage here until we leave?	Nos valises peuvent rester ici jusqu'à notre départ? *noa vahleez puhv rehstay eesee jhewskah notr daypahr?*
Thanks for your _____ hospitality	Merci pour votre hospitalité *mehrsee poor votr ospeetahleetay*

7

Overnight accommodation

Money matters

Money matters

● **In general, banks are open** to the public between 9am and 12 noon and between 2 and 4pm; they are closed on Saturdays. In large city centres they are often open at lunchtime. In tourist areas, the bank can be closed on Monday morning and open on Saturday morning. To exchange currency a proof of identity is usually required. The sign *Change* indicates that money can be exchanged. Hotels and railway stations may also offer exchange facilities but at less favourable rates.

.1 **B**anks

Where can I find a bank/an exchange office around here?	Où puis-je trouver une banque/un bureau de change par ici?
	oo pwee jhuh troovay ewn bohnk/uhn bewroa duh shohnjh pahr eesee?
Where can I cash this traveller's cheque/giro cheque?	Où puis-je encaisser ce chèque de voyage/chèque postal?
	oo pwee jhuh ohnkehssay suh shehk duh vvahyajh/shehk postahl?
Can I cash this...here?	Puis-je encaisser ce...ici?
	pweejh ohnkehssay suh...eesee?
Can I withdraw money on my credit card here?	Puis-je retirer de l'argent avec une carte de crédit?
	pwee jhuh ruhteeray duh lahrjhohn ahvehk ewn kahrt duh kraydee?
What's the minimum/maximum amount?	Quel est le montant minimum/maximum?
	kehl eh luh mohntohn meeneemuhm/mahxseemuhm?
Can I take out less than that?	Puis-je retirer moins?
	pwee jhuh ruhteeray mwahn?
I've had some money transferred here. Has it arrived yet?	J'ai fait virer de l'argent par mandat télégraphique. Est-ce déjà arrivé?
	jhay feh veeray duh lahrjhohn pahr mohndah taylaygrahfeek. ehs dayjhah ahreevay?
These are the details of my bank in the UK	Voici les coordonnées de ma banque au Royaume-Uni
	vwahsee lay koa-ordonay duh mah bohnk oa rwahyoam ewnee
This is my bank/giro account number	Voici mon numéro de compte bancaire/numéro de chèque postal
	vwahsee mawn newmayroa duh kawnt bohnkehr/newmayroa duh shehk postahl
I'd like to change some money	J'aimerais changer de l'argent
	jhehmuhreh shohnjhay duh lahrjhohn
– pounds into...	des livres sterling contre...
	day leevr stehrleeng kawntr...
– dollars into...	des dollars contre...
	day dolahr kawntr...
What's the exchange rate?	Le change est à combien?
	luh shohnjh eh tah kawnbyahn?
Could you give me some small change with it?	Pouvez-vous me donner de la monnaie?
	poovay voo muh donay duh lah moneh?
This is not right	Ce n'est pas exact
	suh neh pah zehgzah.

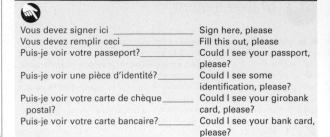

Vous devez signer ici _____	Sign here, please
Vous devez remplir ceci _____	Fill this out, please
Puis-je voir votre passeport?_____	Could I see your passport, please?
Puis-je voir une pièce d'identité?_____	Could I see some identification, please?
Puis-je voir votre carte de chèque postal?	Could I see your girobank card, please?
Puis-je voir votre carte bancaire?_____	Could I see your bank card, please?

.2 Settling the bill

Could you put it on _____ my bill?	Pouvez-vous le mettre sur mon compte?
	poovay voo luh mehtr sewr mawn kawnt?
Does this amount _____ include service?	Est-ce que le service est compris(dans la somme)?
	ehs kuh luh sehrvees eh kawnpree(dohn lah som)?
Can I pay by...?_____	Puis-je payer avec...?
	pwee jhuh payay ahvehk...?
Can I pay by credit card?___	Puis-je payer avec une carte de crédit?
	pwee jhuh payay ahvehk ewn kahrt duh kraydee?
Can I pay by traveller's _____ cheque?	Puis-je payer avec un chèque de voyage?
	pwee jhuh payay ahvehk uhn shehk duh vvahyajh?
Can I pay with foreign _____ currency?	Puis-je vous payer en devises étrangères?
	pwee jhuh voo payay ohn duhveez aytrohnjhehr?
You've given me too _____ much/you haven't given me enough change	Vous m'avez trop/pas assez rendu
	voo mahvay troa/pah zahsay rohndew
Could you check this _____ again, please?	Voulez-vous refaire le calcul?
	voolay voo ruhfehr luh kahlkewl?
Could I have a receipt, _____ please?	Pouvez-vous me donner un reçu/le ticket de caisse?
	poovay voo muh donay uhn ruhsew/luh teekeh duh kehs?
I don't have enough _____ money on me	Je n'ai pas assez d'argent sur moi
	jhuh nay pah zahsay dahrjhohn sewr mwah
This is for you _____	Voilà, c'est pour vous
	vvahlah seh poor voo
Keep the change _____	Gardez la monnaie
	gahrday lah moneh

Nous n'acceptons pas les cartes de _____ crédit/les chèques de voyage/les devises étrangères	We don't accept credit cards/traveller's cheques/foreign currency

Post and telephone

Post and telephone

.1 **P**ost

For giros, see 8 Money matters

● **Post offices** are open from Monday to Friday between 8am and 7pm. In smaller towns the post office closes at lunch. On Saturday they are open between 8am and 12 noon.
Stamps *(timbres)* are also available in a *tabac* (café that sells cigarettes and matches).
The yellow letter box (*boîte aux lettres*) in the street and in the post office has two rates: *tarif normal* (normal rate) and *tarif réduit* (reduced rate).
It is advisable to opt for the *tarif normal*.

colis	télégrammes	timbres
parcels	telegrams	stamps
mandats		
money orders		

Where's...?	Où est...?
	oo eh...?
Where's the post office?	Où est la poste?
	oo eh lah post?
Where's the main post office?	Où est la poste centrale?
	oo eh lah post sohntrahl?
Where's the postbox?	Où est la boîte aux lettres?
	oo eh lah bwaht oa lehtr?
Which counter should I go to...?	Quel est le guichet pour...?
	kehl eh luh gueesheh poor...?
– to send a fax	Quel est le guichet pour les fax?
	kehl eh luh gueesheh poor lay fahx?
– to change money	Quel est le guichet pour changer de l'argent?
	kehl eh luh gueesheh poor shohnjhay duh lahrjhohn?
-to change giro cheques	Quel est le guichet pour les chèques postaux?
	kehl eh luh gueesheh poor lay shehk postoa?
-for a telegraph money order?	Quel est le guichet pour faire un virement postal télégraphique?
	kehl eh luh gueesheh poor fehr uhn veermohn postahl taylaygrahfeek?
Poste restante	Poste restante
	post rehstohnt
Is there any mail for me? My name's...	Y a-t-il du courrier pour moi? Mon nom est...
	ee yah teel dew kooryay poor mwah? mawn nawn eh...

Stamps

What's the postage _____ for a...to...?	Combien faut-il sur une...pour...? *kawnbyahn foa teel sewr ewn...poor...?*
Are there enough _____ stamps on it?	Y a-t-il suffisamment de timbres dessus? *ee yah teel sewfeezahmohn duh tahnbr duhsew?*
I'd like... ...franc stamps____	Je voudrais...timbres à... *jhuh voodreh...tahnbr ah...*
I'd like to send this... _____	Je veux envoyer ce/cette... *jhuh vuh zohnvwahyay suh/seht...*
– express _____	Je veux envoyer ce/cette...en express. *jhuh vuh zohnvwahyay suh/seht...ohn nehxprehs*
– by air mail _____	Je veux envoyer ce/cette...par avion. *jhuh vuh zohnvwahyay suh/seht...pahr ahvyawn*
– by registered mail _____	Je veux envoyer ce/cette...en recommandé. *jhuh vuh zohnvwahyay suh/seht...ohn ruhkomohnday*

Telegram / fax

I'd like to send a _____ telegram to...	J'aimerais envoyer un télégramme à... *jhehmuhreh zohnvwahyay uhn taylaygrahm ah...*
How much is that _____ per word?	C'est combien par mot? *seh kawnbyahn pahr moa?*
This is the text I want____ to send	Voici le texte que je veux envoyer. *vwahsee luh tehxt kuh jhuh vuh zohnvwahyay*
Shall I fill out the form____ myself?	Puis-je remplir le questionnaire moi-même? *pwee jhuh rohnpleer luh kehstyonehr mwah mehm?*
Can I make photocopies/___ send a fax here?	Puis-je faire des photocopies/envoyer un fax ici? *pwee jhuh fehr day foatoakopee/ ohnvwahyay uhn fahx eesee?*

.2 Telephone

See also 1.8 Telephone alphabet

● **All phone booths** offer a direct international service to the UK or the US (00 + country code 44[UK] or 1[US]+ trunk code minus zero + number). In a few cases these are still payable with coins of 1, 5 and 10 francs, but most phone booths will only accept phone cards. These cards (*télécartes*), with 40 or 120 units (*unités*) can be bought at the post office or in a *tabac*. Phone booths do not take incoming calls. Charges can no longer be reversed in France. *A carte globéo* (special card) can be obtained from any office of the telephone company, on presentation of a credit card and identification. Charges are then deducted from the bank account.

When phoning someone in France, you will not be greeted with the subscriber's name, but with *allô* or *allô oui*?

Is there a phone box _____ around here?	Y a-t-il une cabine téléphonique dans le coin?
	ee ah teel ewn kahbeen taylayfoneek dohn luh kwahn?
Could I use your _____ phone, please?	Puis-je utiliser votre téléphone?
	pwee jhuh ewteeleezay votr taylayfon?
Do you have a _____ (city/region)...phone directory?	Avez-vous un annuaire de la ville de.../de la région de...?
	ahvay voo zuhn ahnnewehr duh lah veel duh.../duh lah rayjhyawn duh...?
Where can I get a _____ phone card?	Où puis-je acheter une télécarte?
	oo pwee jhahshtay ewn taylaykahrt?
Could you give me...? _____	Pouvez-vous me donner...?
	poovay voo muh donay...?
– the number for _____ international directory enquiries	Pouvez-vous me donner le numéro des renseignements pour l'étranger?
	poovay voo muh donay luh newmayroa day rohnsehnyuhmohn poor laytrohnjhay?
– the number of room... ___	Pouvez-vous me donner le numéro de la chambre...?
	poovay voo muh donay luh newmayroa duh lah shohnbr...?
– the international _____ access code	Pouvez-vous me donner le numéro international?
	poovay voo muh donay luh newmayroa ahntehrnahsyonahl?
– the country code for...____	Pouvez-vous me donner l'indicatif du pays pour...?
	poovay voo muh donay lahndeekahteef dew payee poor...?
– the trunk code for... _____	Pouvez-vous me donner l'indicatif de...?
	poovay voo muh donay lahndeekahteef duh...?
– the number of... _____	Pouvez-vous me donner le numéro d'abonné de...?
	poovay voo muh donay luh newmayroa dahbonay duh...?
Could you check if this ____ number's correct?	Pouvez-vous vérifier si ce numéro est correct?
	poovay voo vayreefyay see suh newmayroa eh korehkt?
Can I dial international_____ direct?	Puis-je téléphoner en automatique à l'étranger?
	pwee jhuh taylayfonay ohn noatoamahteek ah laytrohnjhay?
Do I have to go through ___ the switchboard?	Dois-je appeler en passant par le standard?
	dwah jhahpuhlay ohn pahsohn pahr luh stohndahr?
Do I have to dial '0' first? __	Dois-je d'abord faire le zéro?
	dwah jhuh dahbor fehr luh zayroa?
Do I have to book _____ my calls?	Dois-je demander ma communication?
	dwah jhuh duhmohnday mah komewneekahsyawn?
Could you dial this _____ number for me, please?	Voulez-vous m'appeler ce numéro?
	voolay voo mahpuhlay suh newmayroa?

Could you put me _____ Voulez-vous me passer.../le poste...?
through to.../extension..., *voolay voo muh pahsay.../luh post...?*
please?

What's the charge per _____ Quel est le prix à la minute?
minute? *kehl eh luh pree ah lah meenewt?*

Have there been any _____ Quelqu'un m'a-t-il appelé?
calls for me? *kehlkuhn mah teel ahpuhlay?*

The conversation

Hello, this is..._____ Allô, ici...
  ahloa, eesee...

Who is this, please? _____ Qui est à l'appareil?
  kee eh tah lahpahrehy?

Is this...? _____ Je parle à...?
  jhuh pahrl ah...?

I'm sorry, I've dialled _____ Pardon, je me suis trompé(e) de numéro
the wrong number *pahrdawn, jhuh muh swee trawnpay duh
  newmayroa.*

I can't hear you _____ Je ne vous entends pas
  jhuh nuh voo zohntohn pah

I'd like to speak to... _____ Je voudrais parler à...
  jhuh voodreh pahrlay ah...

Is there anybody _____ Y a-t-il quelqu'un qui parle l'anglais?
who speaks English? *ee yah teel kehlkuhn kee pahrl lohngleh?*

Extension... please _____ Pouvez-vous me passer le poste...?
  poovay voo muh pahsay luh post...?

Could you ask him/her_____ Voulez-vous demander qu'il/qu'elle me
to call me back? rappelle?
  *voolay voo duhmohnday keel/kehl muh
  rahpehl?*

My name's... _____ Mon nom est...Mon numéro est...
My number's... *mawn nawn eh...mawn newmayroa eh...*

Could you tell him/her _____ Voulez-vous dire que j'ai appelé?
I called? *voolay voo deer kuh jhay ahpuhlay?*

I'll call back tomorrow _____ Je rappellerai demain
  jhuh rahpehluhray duhmahn

On vous demande au téléphone _____	There's a phone call for you
Vous devez d'abord faire le zéro _____	You have to dial '0' first.
Vous avez un instant? _____	One moment, please
Je n'obtiens pas de réponse _____	There's no answer
La ligne est occupée _____	The line's engaged
Vous voulez attendre?_____	Do you want to hold?
Je vous passe la communication_____	Putting you through
Vous vous êtes trompé de numéro _____	You've got a wrong number
Il/elle n'est pas ici en ce moment_____	He's/she's not here right now
Vous pouvez le/la rappeler à... _____	He'll/she'll be back...
C'est le répondeur automatique de... ___	This is the answering machine of...

Shopping

10 **S**hopping

● **Opening times:** Tuesday to Saturday 8/9am-1pm and 2.30-7pm. On Mondays shops are closed in the morning or for the entire day. On Sunday mornings grocers and bakers are usually open, and markets are open until 1pm. Supermarkets and department stores in nearly all cities are open until 8pm once a week. Chemists display the list of *pharmacies de garde* (those open on Sundays and after hours), but you may be charged double in some cities. You may be asked to pay in advance for shoe repairs and dry cleaning.

---

antiquités antiques	grand magasin department store	magasin diététique health food shop
appareils électriques electrical appliances	laverie automatique launderette	marché market
bijoutier jeweller	librairie bookshop	marché aux puces fleamarket
blanchisserie laundry	magasin shop	mercerie draper
boucherie butcher	magasin d'ameublement	pâtisserie cake shop
boulangerie bakery	furniture shop magasin d'appareils	pharmacie chemist
centre commercial shopping centre	photographiques camera shop	poissonnerie fishmonger

charcuterie
delicatessen
	magasin de
	  bicyclettes
		produits ménagers/
		  droguerie

coiffeur (femmes/hommes)	bicycle shop magasin de	household goods quincaillerie
hairdresser (women/men)	bricolage DIY-store	hardware shop réparateur de
cordonnier cobbler	magasin de jouets toy shop	bicyclettes bicycle repairs
crémerie dairy	magasin de disques record shop	salon de beauté beauty parlour

épicerie
grocery store
	magasin de
	  souvenirs
		salon de dégustation
		  de glaces

fleuriste florist	souvenir shop magasin de sport	ice-cream parlour supermarché
fruits et légumes greengrocer	sports shop magasin de vins et	supermarket tabac
galerie marchande shopping arcade	spiritueux off-licence	tobacconist teinturerie dry-cleaner

---

10 .1 **S**hopping conversations

Where can I get...?	Dans quel magasin puis-je acheter...? *dohn kehl mahgahzahn pwee jhahshtay...?*
When does this shop open?	A quelle heure ouvre ce magasin? *ah kehl uhr oovr suh mahgahzahn?*
Could you tell me where the...department is?	Pouvez-vous m'indiquer le rayon de...? *poovay voo mahndeekay luh rayawn duh...?*

83

Could you help me, _____ Pouvez-vous m'aider? Je cherche...
please? I'm looking for... *poovay voo mayday? jhuh shehrsh...*
Do you sell English/ _____ Vendez-vous des journaux
American newspapers? anglais/américains?
vohnday voo day jhoornoa
ohngleh/ahmayreekahn?

👋

On s'occupe de vous? _____ Are you being served?

No, I'd like... _____ Non. J'aimerais...
nawn. jhehmuhreh...

I'm just looking, _____ Je jette un coup d'oeil, si c'est permis
if that's all right *jhuh jheht uhn koo duhy, see seh pehrmee*

👋

Vous désirez autre chose? _____ Anything else?

Yes, I'd also like... _____ Oui, donnez-moi aussi...
wee, donay mwah oasee...
No, thank you. That's all ___ Non, je vous remercie. Ce sera tout
nawn, jhuh voo ruhmehrsee. suh suhrah too
Could you show me...? ____ Pouvez-vous me montrer...?
poovay voo muh mawntray...?
I'd prefer... _____ Je préfère...
jhuh prayfehr...
This is not what I'm _____ Ce n'est pas ce que je cherche
looking for *suh neh pah suh kuh jhuh shehrsh*
Thank you. I'll keep_____ Merci. Je chercherai ailleurs
looking *mehrsee. jhuh shehrshuhray ahyuhr*
Do you have _____ Vous n'avez pas quelque chose de...?
something...? *voo nahvay pah kehlkuh shoaz duh...?*
– less expensive?_____ Vous n'avez pas quelque chose de moins
cher?
voo nahvay pah kehlkuh shoaz duh mwahn
shehr?
– something smaller?_____ Vous n'avez pas quelque chose de plus
petit?
voo nahvay pah kehlkuh shoaz duh plew
puhtee?
– something larger? _____ Vous n'avez pas quelque chose de plus
grand?
voo nahvay pah kehlkuh shoaz duh plew
grohn?
I'll take this one _____ Je prends celui-ci
jhuh prohn suhlwee see
Does it come with _____ Y a-t-il un mode d'emploi avec?
instructions? *ee yah teel uhn mod dohnplwah ahvehk?*
It's too expensive _____ Je le trouve trop cher
jhuh luh troov troa shehr
I'll give you... _____ Je vous offre...
jhuh voo zofr...

Could you keep this for ____ me? I'll come back for it later	Voulez-vous me le mettre de côté? Je reviendrai le chercher tout à l'heure *voolay voo muh luh mehtr duh koatay? jhuh ruhvyahndray luh shehrshay too tah luhr*
Have you got a bag _____ for me, please?	Vous avez un sac? *voo zahvay uhn sahk?*
Could you giftwrap_____ it, please?	Vous pouvez l'emballer dans un papier cadeau? *voo poovay lohnbahlay dohn zuhn pahpyay kahdoa?*

Je suis désolé, nous n'en avons pas ____	I'm sorry, we don't have that
Je suis désolé, le stock est épuisé_____	I'm sorry, we're sold out
Je suis désolé, ce ne sera pas livré_____ avant...	I'm sorry, that won't be in until...
Vous pouvez payer à la caisse _____	You can pay at the cash desk
Nous n'acceptons pas les cartes de ____ crédit	We don't accept credit cards
Nous n'acceptons pas les chèques _____ de voyage	We don't accept traveller's cheques
Nous n'acceptons pas les devises_____ étrangères	We don't accept foreign currency

10 .2 Food

I'd like a hundred_____ grams of..., please	Je voudrais cent grammes de... *jhuh voodreh sohn grahm duh...*
– five hundred grams/ _____ half a kilo of...	Je voudrais une livre de... *jhuh voodreh zewn leevr duh...*
– a kilo of... _____	Je voudrais un kilo de... *jhuh voodreh zuhn keeloa duh...*
Could you...it for me, _____ please?	Vous voulez me le...? *voo voolay muh luh...?*
Could you slice it/ _____ dice it for me, please?	Vous voulez me le couper en tranches/morceaux? *voo voolay muh luh koopay ohn trohnsh/mohrsoa?*
Could you grate it _____ for me, please?	Vous voulez me le râper? *voo voolay muh luh rahpay?*
Can I order it?_____	Puis-je le commander? *pwee jhuh luh komohnday?*
I'll pick it up tomorrow/ ____ at...	Je viendrai le chercher demain/à...heures *jhuh vyahndray luh shehrshay duhmahn/ah...uhr*
Can you eat/drink this? ____	Est-ce mangeable/buvable? *ehs mohnjhahbl/bewvahbl?*
What's in it? _____	Qu'y a-t-il dedans? *kee yah teel duhdohn?*

Shopping

10

I saw something in the ____ window. Shall I point it out?	J'ai vu quelque chose dans la vitrine. Je vous le montre? _jhay vew kehlkuh shoaz dohn lah veetreen. jhuh voo lah mawntr?_
I'd like something to_____ go with this	J'aimerais quelque chose pour aller avec ceci _jhehmuhreh kehlkuh shoaz poor ahlay ahvehk suhsee_
Do you have shoes _____ to match this?	Avez-vous des chaussures de la même couleur que ça? _ahvay voo day shoasewr duh lah mehm kooluhr kuh sah?_
I'm a size...in the UK_____	Je fais du...au Royaume-Uni _jhuh feh dew...oa rwahyoam ewnee_
Can I try this on? _____	Puis-je l'essayer? _pwee jhuh lehsayay?_
Where's the fitting room? __	Où est la cabine d'essayage? _oo eh lah kahbeen dehsayahjh?_
It doesn't fit_____	Cela ne me va pas _suhlah nuh muh vah pah_
This is the right size _____	C'est la bonne taille _seh lah bon tahy_
It doesn't suit me_____	Cela ne me convient pas _suhlah nuh muh kawnvyahn pah_
Do you have this in...? ____	L'avez-vous aussi en...? _lahvay voo zoasee ohn...?_
The heel's too high/low ____	Je trouve le talon trop haut/bas _jhuh troov luh tahlawn troa oa/bah_
Is this/are these _____ genuine leather?	Est-ce/sont-elles en cuir? _eh suh/sawn tehl ohn kweer?_
I'm looking for a..._____ for a...-year-old baby/child	Je cherche un...pour un bébé/enfant de...ans _jhuh shehrsh uhn...poor uhn baybay/ohnhfohn duh...ohn_
I'd like a... ... _____	J'aurais aimé un...de... _jhoareh zaymay uhn... duh..._
– silk _____	J'aurais aimé un...de soie _jhoareh zaymay uhn...duh swah_
– cotton _____	J'aurais aimé un...de coton _jhoareh zaymay uhn...duh koatawn_
– woollen_____	J'aurais aimé un...de laine _jhoareh zaymay uhn...duh lehn_
– linen_____	J'aurais aimé un...de lin _jhoareh zaymay uhn...duh lahn_
What temperature_____ can I wash it at?	A quelle température puis-je le laver? _ah kehl tohnpayrahtewr pwee jhuh luh lahvay?_
Will it shrink in the _____ wash?	Cela rétrécit au lavage? _suhlah raytraysee oa lahvahjh?_

Ne pas repasser	Étendre humide	Laver à la main
Do not iron	Drip dry	Hand wash
Ne pas essorer	Nettoyage à sec	Laver à la machine
Do not spin dry	Dry clean	Machine wash

At the cobbler

Could you mend _____ these shoes?	Pouvez-vous réparer ces chaussures?
	poovay voo raypahray say shoasewr?
Could you put new _____ soles/heels on these?	Pouvez-vous y mettre de nouvelles semelles/nouveaux talons?
	poovay voo zee mehtr duh noovehl suhmehl/noovoa tahlawn?
When will they be _____ ready?	Quand seront-elles prêtes?
	kohn suhrawn tehl preht?
I'd like..., please _____	Je voudrais...
	jhuh voodreh...
– a tin of shoe polish _____	Je voudrais une boîte de cirage
	jhuh voodreh zewn bwaht duh seerahjh
– a pair of shoelaces _____	Je voudrais une paire de lacets
	jhuh voodreh zewn pehr duh lahseh

🔟 .4 Photographs and video

I'd like a film for this _____ camera, please	Je voudrais un rouleau de pellicules pour cet appareil
	jhuh voodreh zuhn rooloa duh payleekewl poor seht ahpahrehy
– a 126 _____ cartridge	Je voudrais une cartouche de cent vingt-six
	jhuh voodreh zewn kahrtoosh duh sohn vahn sees
– a slide film _____	Je voudrais un rouleau de pellicules pour diapositives
	jhuh voodreh zuhn rooloa duh payleekewl poor deeahpoaseeteev
– a film _____	Je voudrais un rouleau de pellicules
	jhuh voodreh zuhn rooloa duh payleekewl
– a videotape _____	Je voudrais une vidéocassette
	jhuh voodreh zewn veedayoakahseht
colour/black and white _____	couleur/noir et blanc
	kooluhr/nwahr ay blohn
super eight _____	super huit mm
	sewpehr wee meeleemehtr
12/24/36 exposures _____	douze/vingt-quatre/trente-six poses
	dooz/vahn kahtr/trohnt see poaz
ASA/DIN number _____	nombre d'ASA/DIN
	nohnbr dahzah/deen
daylight film _____	film pour la lumière du jour
	feelm poor lah lewmyehr dew joor
film for artificial light _____	film pour la lumière artificielle
	feelm poor lah lewmyehr ahrteefeesyehl

Problems

Could you load the _____ film for me, please?
Voulez-vous mettre le film dans l'appareil?
voolay voo mehtr luh feelm dohn lahpahrehy?

Could you take the film _____ out for me, please?
Voulez-vous enlever le film de l'appareil-photo?
voolay voo zohnluhvay luh feelm duh lahpahrehy foatoa?

Should I replace _____ the batteries?
Dois-je changer les piles?
dwah jhuh shohnjhay lay peel?

Could you have a look _____ at my camera, please? It's not working
Voulez-vous jeter un coup d'oeil à mon appareil-photo? Il ne marche plus
voolay voo jhuhtay uhn koo duhy ah mawn nahpahrehy foatoa? eel nuh mahrsh plew

The...is broken _____
Le...est cassé
luh...eh kahssay

The film's jammed _____
La pellicule est bloquée
lah payleekewl eh blokay

The film's broken _____
La pellicule est cassée
lah payleekewl eh kahssay

The flash isn't working _____
Le flash ne marche pas
luh flahsh nuh mahrsh pah

Processing and prints

I'd like to have this film _____ developed/printed, please
Je voudrais faire développer/tirer ce film
jhuh voodreh fehr dayvuhlopay/teeray suh feelm

I'd like...prints from _____ each negative
Je voudrais...tirages de chaque négatif
jhuh voodreh...teerahjh duh shahk naygahteef

glossy/mat _____
brillant/mat
breeyohn/maht

6x9 _____
six sur neuf
sees sewr nuhf

I'd like to re-order _____ these photos
Je veux faire refaire cette photo
jhuh vuh fehr ruhfehr seht foatoa

I'd like to have this _____ photo enlarged
Je veux faire agrandir cette photo
jhuh vuh fehr ahgrohndeer seht foatoa

How much is _____ processing?
Combien coûte le développement?
kawnbyahn koot luh dayvuhlopmohn?

– printing _____
Combien coûte le tirage?
kawnbyahn koot luh teerahjh?

– to re-order _____
Combien coûte la commande supplémentaire?
kawnbyahn koot lah komohnd sewplaymohntehr?

– the enlargement _____
Combien coûte l'agrandissement?
kawnbyahn koot lahgrohndeesmohn?

When will they _____ be ready?
Quand seront-elles prêtes?
kohn suhrawn tehl preht?

Do I have to make an _____ appointment?	Dois-je prendre un rendez-vous? *dwah jhuh prohndr uhn rohnday voo?*
Can I come in straight _____ away?	Pouvez-vous vous occuper de moi immédiatement? *poovay voo voo zokewpay duh mwah eemaydyahtmohn?*
How long will I have _____ to wait?	Combien de temps dois-je attendre? *kawnbyahn duh tohn dwah jhahtohndr?*
I'd like a shampoo/ _____ haircut	Je veux me faire laver/couper les cheveux *jhuh vuh muh fehr lahvay/koopay lay shuhvuh*
I'd like a shampoo for _____ oily/dry hair, please	Je voudrais un shampooing pour cheveux gras/secs *jhuh voodreh zuhn shohnpwahn poor shuhvuh grah/sehk*
an anti-dandruff _____ shampoo	Je voudrais un shampooing anti-pelliculaire *jhuh voodreh zuhn shohnpwahn ohnteepayleekewlehr*
– a shampoo for _____ permed/coloured hair	Je voudrais un shampooing pour cheveux permanentés/colorés *jhuh voodreh zuhn shohnpwahn poor shuhvuh pehrmahnohntay/kohlohray*
– a colour rinse shampoo _____	Je voudrais un shampooing colorant *jhuh voodreh zuhn shohnpwahn kolorohn*
– a shampoo with _____ conditioner	Je voudrais un shampoing avec un soin traitant *jhuh voodreh zuhn shohnpwahn ahvehk uhn swahn trehtohn*
– highlights _____	Je voudrais me faire faire des mèches *jhuh voodreh muh fehr fehr day mehsh*
Do you have a colour _____ chart, please?	Avez-vous une carte de coloration s'il vous plaît? *ahvay voo zewn kahrt duh kolorahsyawn seel voo pleh?*
I want to keep it the _____ same colour	Je veux garder la même couleur *jhuh vuh gahrday lah mehm kooluhr*
I'd like it darker/lighter _____	Je les veux plus sombres/clairs *jhuh lay vuh plew sawmbr/klehr*
I'd like/I don't want _____ hairspray	Je veux de la/ne veux pas de laque *jhuh vuh duh la/nuh vuh pah duh lahk*
– gel _____	Je veux du/ne veux pas de gel *jhuh vuh dew/ nuh vuh pah duh jhehl*
– lotion _____	Je veux de la/ne veux pas de lotion *jhuh vuh duh lah/nuh vuh pah duh loasyawn*
I'd like a short fringe _____	Je veux ma frange courte *jhuh vuh mah frohnjh koort*
Not too short at the _____ back	Je ne veux pas la nuque trop courte *jhuh nuh vuh pah lah newk troa koort*
Not too long here _____	Ici je ne les veux pas trop longs *eesee jhuh nuh lay vuh pah troa lawn*
I'd like/I don't want _____ (many) curls	Je (ne) veux (pas) être (trop) frisée *jhuh (nuh) vuh (pah) ehtr (troa) freezay*

Shopping

10

It needs a little/_____ a lot taken off	Il faut en enlever une petite/grande quantité
	eel foa ohn nohnluhvay ewn puhteet/grohnd kohnteetay
I want a completely _____ different style	Je veux une toute autre coupe
	jhuh vuh zewn toot oatr koop
I'd like it like..._____	Je veux mes cheveux comme...
	jhuh vuh may shuhvuh kom...
– the same as that lady's___	Je veux la même coiffure que cette femme
	jhuh vuh lah mehm kwahfewr kuh seht fahm
– the same as in this photo	Je veux la même coiffure que sur cette photo
	jhuh vuh lah mehm kwahfewr kuh sewr seht foatoa
Could you put the _____ drier up/down a bit?	Pouvez-vous mettre le casque plus haut/plus bas?
	poovay voo mehtr luh kahsk plew oa/plew bah?
I'd like a facial_____	J'aimerais un masque de beauté
	jhehmuhreh zuhn mahsk duh boatay
– a manicure_____	J'aimerais qu'on me fasse les ongles
	jhehmuhreh kawn muh fahs lay zawngl
– a massage _____	J'aimerais un massage
	jhehmuhreh zuhn mahsahjh

Quelle coupe de cheveux_____ désirez-vous?	How do you want it cut?
Quelle coiffure désirez-vous? _____	What style did you have in mind?
Quelle couleur désirez-vous? _____	What colour do you want?
Est-ce la bonne température? _____	Is the temperature all right for you?
Voulez-vous lire quelque chose? _____	Would you like something to read?
Voulez-vous boire quelque chose? _____	Would you like a drink?
C'est ce que vous vouliez?_____	Is this what you had in mind?

Could you trim _____ my fringe?	Pouvez-vous égaliser ma frange?
	poovay voo zaygahleezay mah frohnjh?
– my beard? _____	Pouvez-vous égaliser ma barbe?
	poovay voo zaygahleezay mah bahrb?
– my moustache? _____	Pouvez-vous égaliser ma moustache?
	poovay voo zaygahleezay mah moostahsh?
I'd like a shave, please_____	Pouvez-vous me raser s'il vous plaît?
	poovay voo muh rahzay seel voo pleh?
I'd like a wet shave, _____ please	Je veux être rasé au rasoir à main
	jhuh vuh zehtr rahzay oa rahzwahr ah mahn

At the Tourist Information Centre

11 At the Tourist Information Centre

11 .1 Places of interest

Where's the Tourist Information, please?	Où est l'office de tourisme? *oo eh lofees duh tooreesm?*
Do you have a city map?	Avez-vous un plan de la ville? *ahvay voo zuhn plohn duh lah veel?*
Where is the museum?	Où est le musée? *oo eh luh mewzay?*
Where can I find a church?	Où puis-je trouver une église? *oo pwee jhuh troovay ewn aygleez?*
Could you give me some information about...?	Pouvez-vous me renseigner sur...? *poovay voo muh rohnsehnyay sewr...?*
How much is that?	Combien ça coûte? *kawnbyahn sah koot?*
What are the main places of interest?	Quelles sont les curiosités les plus importantes? *kehl sawn lay kewryoseetay lay plewz ahnportohnt?*
Could you point them out on the map?	Pouvez-vous les indiquer sur la carte? *poovay voo lay zahndeekay sewr lah kahrt?*
What do you recommend?	Que nous conseillez-vous? *kuh noo kawnsehyay voo?*
We'll be here for a few hours	Nous restons ici quelques heures. *noo rehstawn zeesee kehlkuh zuhr.*
– a day	Nous restons ici une journée. *noo rehstawn zeesee ewn jhoornay.*
– a week	Nous restons ici une semaine. *noo rehstawn zeesee ewn suhmehn.*
We're interested in...	Nous sommes intéressés par... *noo som zahntayrehsay pahr...*
Is there a scenic walk around the city?	Pouvons-nous faire une promenade en ville? *poovawn noo fehr ewn promuhnahd ohn veel?*
How long does it take?	Combien de temps dure-t-elle? *kawnbyahn duh tohn dewr tehl?*
Where does it start/end?	Où est le point de départ/d'arrivée? *oo eh luh pwahn duh daypahr/dahreevay?*
Are there any boat cruises here?	Y a-t-il des bateaux-mouches? *ee yah teel day bahtoa moosh?*
Where can we board?	Où pouvons-nous embarquer? *oo poovawn noo zohnbahrkay?*
Are there any bus tours?	Y a-t-il des promenades en bus? *ee yah teel day promuhnahd ohn bews?*
Where do we get on?	Où devons-nous monter? *oo devawn noo mawntay?*
Is there a guide who speaks English?	Y a-t-il un guide qui parle l'anglais? *ee yah teel uhn gueed kee pahrl lohngleh?*
What trips can we take around the area?	Quelles promenades peut-on faire dans la région? *kehl promuhnahd puh tawn fehr dohn lah rayjhyawn?*

Are there any excursions?	Y a-t-il des excursions? *ee yah teel day zehxkewrsyawn?*
Where do they go to?	Où vont-elles? *oo vawn tehl?*
We'd like to go to...	Nous voulons aller à... *noo voolawn zahlay ah...*
How long is the trip?	Combien de temps dure l'excursion? *kawnbyahn duh tohn dewr lehxkewrsyawn?*
How long do we stay in...?	Combien de temps restons-nous à...? *kawnbyahn duh tohn rehstawn noo zah...?*
Are there any guided tours?	Y a-t-il des visites guidées? *ee yah teel day veezeet gueeday?*
How much free time will we have there?	Combien de temps avons-nous de libre? *kawnbyahn duh tohn ahvawn noo duh leebr?*
We want to go hiking	Nous voulons faire une randonnée *noo voolawn fehr ewn rohndonay*
Can we hire a guide?	Pouvons-nous prendre un guide? *poovawn noo prohndr uhn gueed?*
Can I book mountain huts?	Puis-je réserver un refuge? *pwee jhuh rayzehrvay uhn ruhfewjhuh?*
What time does... open/close?	A quelle heure ouvre/ferme...? *ah kehl uhr oovr/fehrm...?*
What days is...open/ closed?	Quels sont les jours d'ouverture/de fermeture...? *kehl sawn lay jhoor doovehrtewr/duh fehrmuhtewr duh...?*
What's the admission price?	Quel est le prix d'entrée? *kehl eh luh pree dohntray?*
Is there a group discount?	Y a-t-il une réduction pour les groupes? *ee yah teel ewn raydewksyawn poor lay groop?*
Is there a child discount?	Y a-t-il une réduction pour les enfants? *ee yah teel ewn raydewksyawn poor lay zohnfohn?*
Is there a discount for pensioners?	Y a-t-il une réduction pour les personnes de plus de soixante-cinq ans? *ee yah teel ewn raydewksyawn poor lay pehrson duh plew duh swahssohnt sahnk ohn?*
Can I take (flash) photos/can I film here?	M'est-il permis de prendre des photos(avec flash)/filmer ici? *meh teel pehrmee duh prohndr day foatoa(ahvehk flahsh)/feelmay eesee?*
Do you have any postcards of...?	Vendez-vous des cartes postales de...? *vohnday voo day kahrt postahl duh...?*
Do you have an English...?	Avez-vous un...en anglais? *ahvay voo zuhn...ohn nohngleh?*
– an English catalogue?	Avez-vous un catalogue en anglais? *ahvay voo zuhn kahtahlog ohn nohngleh?*
– an English programme?	Avez-vous un programme en anglais? *ahvay voo zuhn prograhm ohn nohngleh?*
– an English brochure?	Avez-vous une brochure en anglais? *ahvay voo zewn broshewr ohn nohngleh?*

At the Tourist Information Centre

● **In French theatres** you are usually shown to your seat by an usherette from whom you can buy a programme. It is customary to tip. At the cinema most films are dubbed (*version française*). In large cities subtitled versions are often screened, advertised as *version originale* or *V.O.* If the publicity does not mention *V.O.*, the film will be dubbed. *L'Officiel des spectacles* (an entertainment guide) can be obtained from newspaper kiosks.

Do you have this _____ week's/month's entertainment guide?
Avez-vous le journal des spectacles de cette semaine/de ce mois?
ahvay voo luh jhoornal day spehktahkl duh seht suhmehn/duh suh mwah?

What's on tonight? _____
Que peut-on faire ce soir?
kuh puh tawn fehr suh swahr?

We want to go to... _____
Nous voulons aller au...
noo voolawn zahlay oa...

Which films are _____ showing?
Quels films passe-t-on?
kehl feelm pah stawn?

What sort of film is that?___
Qu'est-ce que c'est comme film?
kehs kuh seh kom feelm?

suitable for all ages _____
pour tous les âges
poor too lay zahjh

not suitable for children under 12/16 years
pour les plus de douze ans/seize ans
poor lay plew duh dooz ohn/sehz ohn

original version _____
version originale
vehrsyawn oreejheenahl

subtitled_____
sous-titré
soo teetray

dubbed_____
doublé
dooblay

Is it a continuous_____ showing?
Est-ce un spectacle permanent?
ehs uhn spehktahkl pehrmahnohn?

What's on at...? _____
Qu'y a-t-il au...?
kee yah teel oa...?

– the theatre? _____
Qu'y a-t-il au théâtre?
kee yah teel oa tayahtr?

– the concert hall? _____
Qu'y a-t-il à la salle des concerts?
kee yah teel ah lah sahl day kawnsehr?

– the opera? _____
Qu'y a-t-il à l'opéra?
kee yah teel ah loapayrah?

Where can I find a good ___ disco around here?
Où se trouve une bonne disco par ici?
oo suh troov ewn bon deeskoa pahr eesee?

Is it members only? _____
Exige-t-on une carte de membre?
ehgzeejh-tawn ewn kahrt duh mohnbr?

Where can I find a good ___ nightclub around here?
Où se trouve une bonne boîte de nuit par ici?
oo suh troov ewn bon bwaht duh nwee pahr eesee?

Is it evening wear only? ___
La tenue de soirée, est-elle obligatoire?
lah tuhnew duh swahray, eh tehl obleegahtwahr?

Should I/we dress up? _____
La tenue de soirée, est-elle souhaitée?
lah tuhnew duh swahray ehtehl sooehtay?

What time does the _____ show start?	A quelle heure commence la représentation? *ah kehl uhr komohns lah ruhprayzohntahsyawn?*
When's the next soccer _____ match?	Quand est le prochain match de football? *kohn teh luh proshahn mahtch duh footbohl?*
Who's playing?_____	Qui joue contre qui? *kee jhoo kawntr kee?*
I'd like an escort for _____ tonight. Could you arrange that for me?	Je veux une hôtesse pour ce soir. *jhuh vuh zewn oatehs poor suh swahr.* Pouvez-vous arranger ça? *poovay voo zahrohnjhay sah?*

11 .3 Booking tickets

Could you book some _____ tickets for us?	Pouvez-vous nous faire une réservation? *poovay voo noo fehr ewn rayzehrvahsyawn?*
We'd like to book... _____ seats/a table...	Nous voulons...places/une table... *noo voolawn...plahs/ewn tahbl...*
– in the stalls_____	Nous voulons...places à l'orchestre. *noo voolawn...plahs ah lorkehstr*
– on the balcony _____	Nous voulons...places au balcon. *noo voolawn...plahs oa bahlkawn*
– box seats _____	Nous voulons...places dans les loges. *noo voolawn...plahs dohn lay lojh*
– a table at the front_____	Nous voulons...une table à l'avant. *noo voolawn...ewn tahbl ah lahvohn*
– in the middle_____	Nous voulons...places au milieu. *noo voolawn...plahs oa meelyuh*
– at the back _____	Nous voulons...places à l'arrière. *noo voolawn...plahs ah lahryehr*
Could I book...seats for _____ the...o'clock performance?	Puis-je réserver...places pour la représentation de...heures? *pwee jhuh rayzehrvay...plahs poor lah ruhprayzohntahsyawn duh...uhr?*
Are there any seats left _____ for tonight?	Reste-t-il encore des places pour ce soir? *rehst-uh-teel ohnkor day plahs poor suh swahr?*
How much is a ticket? _____	Combien coûte un billet? *kawnbyahn koot uhn beeyeh?*
When can I pick the _____ tickets up?	Quand puis-je venir chercher les billets? *kohn pwee jhuh vuhneer shehrshay lay beeyeh?*
I've got a reservation _____	J'ai réservé *jhay rayzehrvay*
My name's... _____	Mon nom est... *mawn nawn eh...*

Vous voulez réserver pour quelle _____ représentation?	Which performance do you want to book for?
Où voulez-vous vous asseoir? _____	Where would you like to sit?
Tout est vendu_____	Everything's sold out
Il ne reste que des places debout _____	It's standing room only
Il ne reste que des places_____ au balcon	We've only got balcony seats left
Il ne reste que des places au_____ poulailler	We've only got seats left in the gallery
Il ne reste que des places_____ d'orchestre	We've only got stalls seats left
Il ne reste que des places à l'avant _____	We've only got seats left at the front
Il ne reste que des places à l'arrière _____	We've only got seats left at the back
Combien de places voulez-vous?_____	How many seats would you like?
Vous devez venir chercher les billets _____ avant...heures	You'll have to pick up the tickets before...o'clock
Puis-je voir vos billets? _____	Tickets, please
Voici votre place _____	This is your seat
Vous n'êtes pas aux bonnes places _____	You're in the wrong seats

Sports

12 Sports

12.1 Sporting questions

Where can we... around here?	Où pouvons-nous...?
	oo poovawn noo...?
Is there a... around here?	Y a-t-il uhn...dans les environs?
	ee yah teel uhn...dohn lay zohnveerawn?
Can I hire a...here?	Puis-je louer un...ici?
	pwee jhuh looay uhn...eesee?
Can I take...lessons?	Puis-je prendre des cours de...?
	pwee jhuh prohndr day koor duh...?
How much is that per hour/per day/a turn?	Quel est le prix à l'heure/à la journée/à chaque fois?
	kehl eh luh pree ah luhr/ah lah jhoornay/ah shahk fwah?
Do I need a permit for that?	A-t-on besoin d'un permis?
	ah tawn buhzwahn duhn pehrmee?
Where can I get the permit?	Où puis-je obtenir le permis?
	oo pwee jhuh obtuhneer luh pehrmee?

12.2 By the waterfront

Is it a long way to the sea still?	La mer, est-elle encore loin?
	lah mehr eh tehl ohnkor lwahn?
Is there a...around here?	Y a-t-il un...dans les environs?
	ee yah teel uhn...dohn lay zohnveerawn?
– a public swimming pool	Y a-t-il une piscine dans les environs?
	ee yah teel ewn peeseen dohn lay zohnveerawn?
– a sandy beach	Y a-t-il une plage de sable dans les environs?
	ee yah teel ewn plahj duh sahbl dohn lay zohnveerawn?
– a nudist beach	Y a-t-il une plage pour nudistes dans les environs?
	ee yah teel ewn plahj poor newdeest dohn lay zohnveerawn?
– mooring	Y a-t-il un embarcadère pour les bateaux dans les environs?
	ee yah teel uhn nohnbahrkahdehr poor lay bahtoa dohn lay zohnveerawn?
Are there any rocks here?	Y a-t-il aussi des rochers ici?
	ee yah teel oasee day roshay eesee?
When's high/low tide?	Quand est la marée haute/basse?
	kohn teh lah mahray oat/bahs?
What's the water temperature?	Quelle est la température de l'eau?
	kehl eh lah tohnpayratewr duh loa?
Is it (very) deep here?	Est-ce (très) profond ici?
	ehs (treh) proafawn eesee?
Can you stand here?	A-t-on pied ici?
	ah tawn pyay eesee?
Is it safe to swim here?	Peut-on nager en sécurité ici?
	puh tawn nahjhay ohn saykewreetay eesee?
Are there any currents?	Y a-t-il des courants?
	ee yah teel day koorohn?

Are there any rapids/ _____ waterfalls in this river?	Est-ce que cette rivière a des courants rapides/des chutes d'eau?
	ehs kuh seht reevyehr ah day koorohn rahpeed/day shewt doa?
What does that flag/ _____ buoy mean?	Que signifie ce drapeau/cette bouée là-bas?
	kuh seenyeefee suh drahpoa/seht booway lah bah?
Is there a life guard _____ on duty here?	Y a-t-il un maître nageur qui surveille?
	ee yah teel uhn mehtr nahjhuhr kee sewrvehy?
Are dogs allowed here? _____	Les chiens sont admis ici?
	lay shyahn sawn tahdmee eesee?
Is camping on the _____ beach allowed?	Peut-on camper sur la plage?
	puh tawn kohnpay sewr lah plahjh?
Are we allowed to _____ build a fire here?	Peut-on faire un feu ici?
	puh tawn fehr uhn fuh eesee?

Danger	Pêche interdite	Baignade interdite
Danger	No fishing	No swimming
Pêche	Surf interdit	Seulement avec
Fishing water	No surfing	permis
		Permits only

🕛 .3 In the snow

Can I take ski lessons _____ here?	Puis-je prendre des leçons de ski?
	pwee jhuh prohndr day luhsawn duh skee?
for beginners/advanced _____	pour débutants/initiés
	poor daybewtohn/eeneesyay
How large are the _____ groups?	Quelle est la taille des groupes?
	kehl eh lah tahy day groop?
What language are _____ the classes in?	En quelle langue donne-t-on les leçons de ski?
	ohn kehl lohng don tawn lay luhsawn duh skee?
I'd like a lift pass, _____ please	Je voudrais un abonnement pour les remontées mécaniques.
	jhuh voodreh zuhn nahbonmohn poor lay ruhmawntay maykahneek
Must I give you a _____ passport photo?	Dois-je donner une photo d'identité?
	dwah jhuh donay ewn foatoa deedohnteetay?
Where can I have a _____ passport photo taken?	Où puis-je faire faire une photo d'identité?
	oo pwee jhuh fehr fehr ewn foatoa deedohnteetay?
Where are the _____ beginners' slopes?	Où sont les pistes de ski pour débutants?
	oo sawn lay peest duh skee poor daybewtohn?
Are there any runs for _____ cross-country skiing?	Y a-t-il des pistes de ski de fond dans les environs?
	ee yah teel day peest duh skee duh fawn dohn lay zohnveerawn?

Sports

12

Have the cross-country runs been marked?	Les pistes de ski de fond, sont-elles indiquées?
	lay peest duh skee duh fawn, sawn tehl ahndeekay?
Are the...in operation?	Est-ce que les...marchent?
	ehs kuh lay...mahrsh?
– the ski lifts	Est-ce que les remontées mécaniques marchent?
	ehs kuh lay ruhmawntay maykahneek mahrsh?
– the chair lifts	Est-ce que les télésièges marchent?
	ehs kuh lay taylaysyehjh mahrsh?
Are the slopes usable?	Est-ce que les pistes sont ouvertes?
	ehs kuh lay peest sawn toovehrt?
Are the cross-country runs usable?	Est-ce que les pistes de ski de fond sont ouvertes?
	ehs kuh lay peest duh skee duh fawn sawn toovehrt?

Sickness

13 Sickness

13.1 Call (fetch) the doctor

Could you call/fetch a_____ doctor quickly, please?	Voulez-vous vite appeler/aller chercher un médecin s'il vous plaît?
	voolay voo veet ahpuhlay/ahlay shehrshay uhn maydsahn seel voo pleh?
When does the doctor _____ have surgery?	Quand est-ce que le médecin reçoit?
	kohn tehs kuh luh maydsahn ruhswah?
When can the doctor _____ come?	Quand est-ce que le médecin peut venir?
	kohn tehs kuh luh maydsahn puh vuhneer?
I'd like to make an_____ appointment to see the doctor	Pouvez-vous me prendre un rendez-vous chez le médecin?
	poovay voo muh prohndr uhn rohnday voo shay luh maydsahn?
I've got an appointment ___ to see the doctor at...	J'ai un rendez-vous chez le médecin à...heures
	jhay uhn rohnday voo shay luh maydsahn a...uhr
Which doctor/chemist _____ has night/weekend duty?	Quel médecin/Quelle pharmacie est de garde cette nuit/ce week-end?
	kehl maydsahn/kehl fahrmahsee eh duh gahrd seht nwee/suh week-ehnd?

13.2 Patient's ailments

I don't feel well _____	Je ne me sens pas bien
	jhuh nuh muh sohn pah byahn
I'm dizzy_____	J'ai des vertiges
	jhay day vehrteejh
– ill_____	Je suis malade
	jhuh swee mahlahd
– sick_____	J'ai mal au coeur
	jhay mahl oa kuhr
I've got a cold_____	Je suis enrhumé(e)
	jhuh swee zohnrewmay
It hurts here _____	J'ai mal ici
	jhay mahl eesee
I've been throwing up ____	J'ai vomi
	jhay vomee
I've got... _____	Je souffre de...
	jhuh soofr duh...
I'm running a _____ temperature	J'ai de la fièvre
	jhayduh lah fyehvr
I've been stung by_____ a wasp.	J'ai été piqué(e) par une guêpe
	jhay aytay peekay pahr ewn gehp
I've been stung by an_____ insect	J'ai été piqué(e) par un insecte
	jhay aytay peekay pahr uhn nahnsehkt
I've been bitten by _____ a dog	J'ai été mordu(e) par un chien
	jhay aytay mordew pahr uhn shyahn
I've been stung by_____ a jellyfish	J'ai été piqué(e) par une méduse
	jhay aytay peekay pahr ewn maydewz
I've been bitten by _____ a snake	J'ai été mordu(e) par un serpent
	jhay aytay mordew pahr uhn sehrpohn

I've been bitten by _____ an animal	J'ai été mordu(e) par un animal *jhay aytay mordew pahr uhn nahneemahl*
I've cut myself _____	Je me suis coupé(e) *jhuh muh swee koopay*
I've burned myself _____	Je me suis brûlé(e) *jhuh muh swee brewlay*
I've grazed myself_____	Je me suis égratigné(e) *jhuh muh swee zaygrahteenyay*
I've had a fall _____	Je suis tombé(e) *jhuh swee tawnbay*
I've sprained my ankle____	Je me suis foulé(e) la cheville *jhuh muh swee foolay lah shuhveey*
I've come for the _____ morning-after pill	Je viens pour la pilule du lendemain *jhuh vyahn poor lah peelewl dew lohndmahn*

🤝 .3 The consultation

Quels sont vos symptômes?_____	What seems to be the problem?
Depuis combien de temps avez-vous____ ces symptômes?	How long have you had these symptoms?
Avez-vous eu ces symptômes_____ auparavant?	Have you had this trouble before?
Avez-vous de la fièvre?_____	How high is your temperature?
Déshabillez-vous s'il vous plaît? _____	Get undressed, please
Pouvez-vous vous mettre torse nu? _____	Strip to the waist, please
Vous pouvez vous déshabiller là-bas.____	You can undress there
Pouvez-vous remonter la manche de____ votre bras gauche/droit?	Roll up your left/right sleeve, please
Allongez-vous ici _____	Lie down here, please
Ceci vous fait mal?_____	Does this hurt?
Aspirez et expirez profondément _____	Breathe deeply
Ouvrez la bouche _____	Open your mouth

Patient's medical history

I'm a diabetic _____	Je suis diabétique *jhuh swee dyahbayteek*
I have a heart condition____	Je suis cardiaque *jhuh swee kahrdyahk*
I have asthma_____	J'ai de l'asthme *jhay duh lahsm*
I'm allergic to... _____	Je suis allergique à... *jhuh swee zahlehrjheek ah...*
I'm...months pregnant _____	Je suis enceinte de...mois *jhuh swee zohnsahnt duh...mwah*
I'm on a diet _____	Je suis au régime *jhuh swee zoa rayjheem*
I'm on medication/the pill__	Je prends des médicaments/la pilule *jhuh prohn day maydeekahmohn/lah peelewl*

Sickness

13

I've had a heart attack _____ J'ai déjà eu une crise cardiaque
once before *jhay dayjhah ew ewn kreez kahrdyahk*

I've had a(n)...operation ___ J'ai été opéré(e) de...
jhay aytay oapayray duh...

I've been ill recently _____ Je viens d'être malade
jhuh vyahn dehtr mahlahd

I've got an ulcer_____ J'ai un ulcère à l'estomac
jhay uhn newlsehr ah lehstomah

I've got my period_____ J'ai mes règles
jhay may rehgl

Avez-vous des allergies? _____ Do you have any allergies?
Prenez-vous des médicaments?_____ Are you on any
medication?

Suivez-vous un régime? _____ Are you on a diet?
Etes-vous enceinte? _____ Are you pregnant?
Etes-vous vacciné(e) contre Have you had a tetanus
le tétanos? _____ injection?

The diagnosis

Is it contagious?_____ Est-ce contagieux?
ehs kawntahjhyuh?

How long do I have to _____ Combien de temps dois-je rester...?
stay...? *kawnbyahn duh tohn dwah jhuh rehstay...?*

– in bed _____ Combien de temps dois-je rester au lit?
*kawnbyahn duh tohn dwah jhuh rehstay oa
lee?*

– in hospital _____ Combien de temps dois-je rester à
l'hôpital?
*kawnbyahn duh tohn dwah jhuh rehstay ah
loapeetahl?*

Ce n'est rien de grave _____ It's nothing serious
Vous vous êtes cassé le/la... _____ Your...is broken
Vous vous êtes foulé le/la... _____ You've sprained
your...
Vous vous êtes déchiré le/la..._____ You've got a torn...
Vous avez une inflammation_____ You've got an
inflammation
Vous avez une crise d'appendicite_____ You've got appendicitis
Vous avez une bronchite _____ You've got bronchitis
Vous avez une maladie vénérienne ____ You've got a venereal
disease
Vous avez une grippe _____ You've got the flu
Vous avez eu une crise cardiaque _____ You've had a heart
attack
Vous avez une infection _____ You've got an infection
(virale/bactérielle) (viral/bacterial)
Vous avez une pneumonie_____ You've got pneumonia

Vous avez un ulcère à l'estomac _____	You've got an ulcer
Vous vous êtes froissé un muscle _____	You've pulled a muscle
Vous avez une infection vaginale _____	You've got a vaginal infection
Vous avez une intoxication alimentaire _____	You've got food poisoning
Vous avez une insolation _____	You've got sunstroke
Vous êtes allergique à... _____	You're allergic to...
Vous êtes enceinte _____	You're pregnant
Je veux faire analyser votre sang/urine/vos selles _____	I'd like to have your blood/urine/stools tested
Il faut faire des points de suture _____	It needs stitching
Je vous envoie à un spécialiste/l'hôpital _____	I'm referring you to a specialist/sending you to hospital.
Il faut faire des radios _____	You'll need to have some x-rays taken
Voulez-vous reprendre place un petit instant dans la salle d'attente? _____	Could you wait in the waiting room, please?
Il faut vous opérer _____	You'll need an operation

Do I have to go on a special diet? _____	Dois-je suivre un régime? _dwah jhuh sweevr uhn rayjheem?_
Am I allowed to travel? _____	Puis-je voyager? _pwee jhuh vwahyahjhay?_
Can I make a new appointment? _____	Puis-je prendre un autre rendez-vous? _pwee jhuh prohndr uhn noatr rohnday voo?_
When do I have to come back? _____	Quand dois-je revenir? _kohn dwah jhuh ruhvuhneer?_
I'll come back tomorrow _____	Je reviendrai demain _jhuh ruhvyahndray duhmahn_

Vous devez revenir demain /dans...jours _____	Come back tomorrow/in...days' time

13 .4 Medication and prescriptions

How do I take this medicine? _____	Comment dois-je prendre ces médicaments? _komohn dwah jhuh prohndr say maydeekahmohn?_
How many capsules/ drops/injections/spoonfuls/ tablets each time? _____	Combien de capsules/gouttes/piqûres/ cuillères/comprimés à chaque fois? _kawnbyahn duh kahpsewl/goot/peekewr/ kweeyehr/kawnpreemay ah shahk fwah?_
How many times a day? _____	Combien de fois par jour? _kawnbyahn duh fwah pahr jhoor?_
I've forgotten my medication. At home I take... _____	J'ai oublié mes médicaments. A la maison je prends... _jhay oobleeyay may maydeekahmohn. ah lah mehzawn jhuh prohn..._
Could you make out a prescription for me? _____	Pouvez-vous me faire une ordonnance? _poovay voo muh fehr ewn ordonohns?_

Je vous prescris un antibiotique/un _____ sirop/un tranquillisant/un calmant		I'm prescribing antibiotics/a mixture/a tranquillizer/pain killer
Vous devez rester au calme_____		Have lots of rest
Vous ne devez pas sortir _____		Stay indoors
Vous devez rester au lit_____		Stay in bed

avaler entièrement swallow whole	cuillerées (...à soupe/...à café) spoonfuls (tablespoons/ teaspoons)	pendant...jours for...days
avant chaque repas before meals		piqûres injections
capsules capsules	dissoudre dans l'eau dissolve in water	pommade ointment
la prise de ce médicament peut rendre dangereuse la conduite automobile this medication impairs your driving	enduire rub on	prendre take
	finir le traitement finish the course	toutes les...heures every...hours
	...fois par jour ...times a day	uniquement pour usage externe not for internal use
comprimés tablets	gouttes drops	

13 .5 At the dentist's

Do you know a good _____ dentist?	Connaissez-vous un bon dentiste? *konehsay voo zuhn bawn dohnteest?*
Could you make a _____ dentist's appointment for me? It's urgent	Pouvez-vous me prendre un rendez-vous chez le dentiste? C'est urgent *poovay voo muh prohndr uhn rohnday voo shay luh dohnteest? seh tewrjhohn*
Can I come in today,_____ please?	Puis-je venir aujourd'hui s'il vous plaît? *pwee jhuh vuhneer oajhoordwee seel voo pleh?*
I have (terrible)_____ toothache	J'ai une rage de dents/un mal de dents(épouvantable) *jhay ewn rahjh duh dohn/uhn mahl duh dohn (aypoovohntahbl)*
Could you prescribe/ _____ give me a painkiller?	Pouvez-vous me prescrire/donner un calmant? *poovay voo muh prehskreer/donay uhn kahlmohn?*
A piece of my tooth _____ has broken off	Ma dent s'est cassée *mah dohn seh kahssay*
My filling's come out _____	Mon plombage est parti *mawn plawnbahjh eh pahrtee*
I've got a broken crown_____	Ma couronne est cassée *mah kooron eh kahssay*
I'd like/I don't want a _____ local anaesthetic	Je (ne) veux (pas) une anesthésie locale *jhuh (nuh) vuh (paz) ewn ahnehstayzee lokahl*

Sickness

Can you do a makeshift repair job?	Pouvez-vous me soigner de façon provisoire? *poovay voo muh swahnyay duh fahsawn proveezwahr?*
I don't want this tooth pulled	Je ne veux pas que cette dent soit arrachée *jhuh nuh vuh pah kuh seht dohn swaht ahrahshay*
My dentures are broken. Can you fix them?	Mon dentier est cassé. Pouvez-vous le réparer? *mawn dohntyay eh kahssay. poovay voo luh raypahray?*

🖐

Quelle dent/molaire vous fait mal?	Which tooth hurts?
Vous avez un abcès	You've got an abscess
Je dois faire une dévitalisation	I'll have to do a root canal
Je vais vous faire une anesthésie locale	I'm giving you a local anaesthetic
Je dois plomber/extraire/polir cette dent	I'll have to fill/pull/file down this tooth
Je dois utiliser la roulette	I'll have to drill
Ouvrez bien la bouche	Open wide, please
Fermez la bouche	Close your mouth, please
Rincez	Rinse, please
Sentez-vous encore la douleur?	Does it hurt still?

14

In trouble

14.1 Asking for help

Help!	Au secours! *oa suhkoor!*
Fire!	Au feu! *oa fuh!*
Police!	Police! *pohlees!*
Quick!	Vite! *veet!*
Danger!	Danger! *dohnjhay*
Watch out!	Attention! *ahtohnsyawn!*
Stop!	Stop! *stop!*
Be careful!	Prudence! *prewdohns!*
Don't!	Arrêtez! *ahrehtay!*
Let go!	Lâchez! *lahshay!*
Stop that thief!	Au voleur! *oa voluhr!*
Could you help me, please?	Voulez-vous m'aider? *voolay voo mayday?*
Where's the police station/emergency exit/fire escape?	Où est le poste de police/la sortie de secours/l'escalier de secours? *oo eh luh post duh polees/lah sortoe duh suhkoor/lehskahlyay duh suhkoor?*
Where's the nearest fire extinguisher?	Où y a-t-il un extincteur? *oo ee yah teel uhn nehxtahnktuhr?*
Call the fire brigade!	Prévenez les sapeurs-pompiers! *prayvuhnay lay sahpuhr pawnpyay!*
Call the police!	Appelez la police! *ahpuhlay lah polees!*
Call an ambulance!	Appelez une ambulance! *ahpuhlay ewn ohnbewlohns!*
Where's the nearest phone?	Où est le téléphone le plus proche? *oo eh luh taylayfon luh plew prosh?*
Could I use your phone?	Puis-je utiliser votre téléphone? *pwee jhuh ewteeleezay votr taylayfon?*
What's the emergency number?	Quel est le numéro d'urgence? *kehl eh luh newmayroa dewrjhohns?*
What's the number for the police?	Quel est le numéro de téléphone de la police? *kehl eh luh newmayroa duh taylayfon duh lah polees?*

14.2 Loss

I've lost my purse/_____ wallet	J'ai perdu mon porte-monnaie/portefeuille
	jhay pehrdew mawn port moneh/portfuhy
I lost my...yesterday _____	Hier j'ai oublié mon/ma...
	yehr jhay oobleeay mawn/mah...
I left my...here _____	J'ai laissé mon/ma...ici
	jhay layssay mawn/mah...eesee
Did you find my...? _____	Avez-vous trouvé mon/ma...?
	ahvay voo troovay mawn/mah...?
It was right here_____	Il était là
	eel ayteh lah
It's quite valuable _____	C'est un objet de valeur
	seh tuhn nobjheh duh vahluhr
Where's the lost_____ property office?	Où est le bureau des objets trouvés?
	oo eh luh bewroa day zobjheh troovay?

14.3 Accidents

There's been an accident __	Il y a eu un accident
	eel ee yah ew uhn nahkseedohn
Someone's fallen into _____ the water	Quelqu'un est tombé dans l'eau
	kehlkuhn eh tawnbay dohn loa
There's a fire_____	Il y a un incendie.
	eel ee yah uhn nahnsohndee
Is anyone hurt? _____	Y a-t-il quelqu'un de blessé?
	ee yah teel kehlkuhn duh blehssay?
Some people have _____ been/no one's been injured	Il (n)y a des(pas de) blessés
	eel (n)ee yah day(pah duh) blehssay
There's someone in _____ the car/train still	Il y a encore quelqu'un dans la voiture/le train
	eel ee ah ohnkor kehlkuhn dohn lah vwahtewr/luh trahn
It's not too bad. Don't_____ worry	Ce n'est pas si grave. Ne vous inquiétez pas
	suh neh pah see grahv. nuh voo zahnkyaytay pah
Leave everything the _____ way it is, please	Ne touchez à rien s'il vous plaît
	nuh tooshay ah ryahn seel voo pleh
I want to talk to the_____ police first	Je veux d'abord parler à la police
	jhuh vuh dahbor pahrlay ah lah polees
I want to take a _____ photo first	Je veux d'abord prendre une photo
	jhuh vuh dahbor prohndr ewn foatoa
Here's my name_____ and address	Voici mon nom et mon adresse
	vwahsee mawn nawn ay mawn nahdrehs
Could I have your _____ name and address?	Puis-je connaître votre nom et votre adresse?
	pwee jhuh konehtr votr nawn ay votr ahdrehs?

In trouble

14

Could I see some ___ identification/your insurance papers?	Puis-je voir vos papiers d'identité/papiers d'assurance?
	pwee jhuh vwahr voa pahpyay deedohnteetay/pahpyay dahsewrohns?
Will you act as a ___ witness?	Voulez-vous être témoin?
	voolay voo zehtr taymwahn?
I need the details for ___ the insurance	Je dois avoir les données pour l'assurance.
	jhuh dwah zahvwahr lay donay poor lahsewrohns
Are you insured? ___	Etes-vous assuré?
	eht voo zahsewray?
Third party or ___ comprehensive?	Responsabilité civile ou tous risques?
	rehspawnsahbeeleetay seeveel oo too reesk?
Could you sign here, ___ please?	Voulez-vous signer ici?
	voolay voo seenyay eesee?

🄌 .4 Theft

I've been robbed ___	On m'a volé.
	awn mah volay
My...has been stolen ___	Mon/ma...a été volé(e).
	mawn/mah...ah aytay volay
My car's been ___ broken into	On a cambriolé ma voiture.
	awn nah kohnbreeolay mah vwahtewr

🄌 .5 Missing person

I've lost my child/ ___ grandmother	J'ai perdu mon enfant/ma grand-mère
	jhay pehrdew mawn nohnfohn/mah grohnmehr
Could you help me ___ find him/her?	Voulez-vous m'aider à le/la chercher?
	voolay voo mayday ah luh/lah shehrshay?
Have you seen a ___ small child?	Avez-vous vu un petit enfant?
	ahvay voo vew uhn puhtee tohnfohn?
He's/she's...years old ___	Il/elle a...ans.
	eel/ehl ah...ohn
He's/she's got ___ short/long/blond/red/ brown/black/grey/curly/ straight/frizzy hair	Il/elle a les cheveux courts/longs/blonds/roux/bruns/noirs/gris/bouclés/raides/frisés
	eel/ehl ah lay shuhvuh koor/lawn/blawn/roo/bruhn/nwahr/gree rehd/freezay
with a ponytail ___	avec une queue de cheval
	ahvehk ewn kuh duh shuhvahl
with plaits ___	avec des nattes
	ahvehk day naht
in a bun ___	avec un chignon
	ahvehk uhn sheenyawn
He's/she's got ___ blue/brown/green eyes	Il/elle a les yeux bleus/bruns/verts
	eel/ehl ah lay zyuh bluh/bruhn/vehr
He's wearing swimming ___ trunks/mountaineering boots	Il porte un maillot de bain/des chaussures de montagne.
	eel port uhn mahyoa duh bahn/day shoasewr duh mawntahnyuh

In trouble

🄌

with/without glasses/ _____ a bag	avec/sans lunettes/un sac *ahvehk/sohn lewneht/uhn sahk*
tall/short_____	grand(e)/petit(e) *grohn(d)/puhtee(t)*
This is a photo of _____ him/her	Voici une photo de lui/d'elle. *vwahsee ewn foatoa duh lwee/dehl*
He/she must be lost _____	Il/elle s'est certainement égaré(e) *eel/ehl seh sehrtehnmohn aygahray*

🖐 .6 The police

An arrest

Vos papiers de voiture s'il vous plaît._____	Your registration papers, please
Vous rouliez trop vite _____	You were speeding
Vous êtes en stationnement interdit _____	You're not allowed to park here
Vous n'avez pas mis d'argent dans le ___ parcmètre	You haven't put money in the meter
Vos phares ne marchent pas_____	Your lights aren't working
Vous avez une contravention _____ de...francs	That's a...franc fine
Vous voulez payer immédiatement?_____	Do you want to pay on the spot?
Vous devez payer immédiatement _____	You'll have to pay on the spot

I don't speak French _____	Je ne parle pas français. *jhuh nuh pahrl pah frohnseh*
I didn't see the sign _____	Je n'ai pas vu ce panneau. *jhuh nay pah vew suh pahnoa*
I don't understand_____ what it says	Je ne comprends pas ce qu'il y est écrit. *jhuh nuh kawnprohn pah suh keel ee yeh taykree*
I was only doing..._____ kilometres an hour	Je ne roulais qu'à...kilomètres à l'heure. *jhuh nuh rooleh kah...keeloamehtr ah luhr*
I'll have my car checked ___	Je vais faire réviser ma voiture. *jhuh veh fehr rayveezay mah vwahtewr*
I was blinded by _____ oncoming lights	J'ai été aveuglé(e) par une voiture en sens inverse. *jhay aytay ahvuhglay pahr ewn vwahtewr ohn sohns ahnvehrs*

In trouble

14

At the police station

Où est-ce arrivé?	Where did it happen?
Qu'avez-vous perdu?	What's missing?
Qu'a-t-on volé?	What's been taken?
Puis-je voir vos papiers d'identité?	Could I see some identification?
A quelle heure est-ce arrivé?	What time did it happen?
Qui est en cause?	Who was involved?
Y a-t-il des témoins?	Are there any witnesses?
Voulez-vous remplir ceci?	Fill this out, please
Signez ici s'il vous plaît	Sign here, please
Voulez-vous un interprète?	Do you want an interpreter?

I want to report a collision/missing person/rape
Je viens faire la déclaration d'une collision/d'une disparition/d'un viol
jhuh vyahn fehr lah dayklahrasyawn dewn koleezyawn/dewn deespahreesyawn/duhn vyol

Could you make out a report, please?
Voulez-vous faire un rapport?
voolay voo fehr uhn rahpor?

Could I have a copy for the insurance?
Puis-je avoir une copie pour l'assurance?
pwee jhahvwahr ewn kopee poor lahsewrohns?

I've lost everything
J'ai tout perdu
jhay too pehrdew

I'd like an interpreter
J'aimerais un interprète
jhehmuhreh zuhn nahntehrpreht

I'm innocent
Je suis innocent(e)
jhuh swee zeenosohn(t)

I don't know anything about it
Je ne sais rien
jhuh nuh seh ryahn

I want to speak to someone from the British consulate
Je veux parler à quelqu'un du consulat britannique
jhuh vuh pahrlay ah kehlkuhn dew kawnsewlah breetahneek

I need to see someone from the British embassy
Je dois parler à quelqu'un de l'ambassade britannique
jhuh dwah pahrlay ah kehlkuhn duh lohnbahsahd breetahneek

I want a lawyer who speaks English
Je veux un avocat qui parle anglais
jhuh vuh uhn nahvokah kee pahrl ohngleh

In trouble

113

15

Word list

Word list English - French

● **This word list** is meant to supplement the previous chapters.
Nouns are always accompanied by the French definite article in order
to indicate whether it is a masculine (le) or feminine (la) word. In the
case of an abbreviated article (l'), the gender is indicated by (m.) or (f.).
In a number of cases, words not contained in this list can be found
elsewhere in this book, namely alongside the diagrams of the car, the
bicycle and the tent. Many food terms can be found in the French-
English list in 4.7.

A

about	environ	*ohnveerawn*
above	au-dessus	*oadsew*
abroad	l'étranger (m.)	*laytrohnjhay*
accident	l'accident (m.)	*lahkseedohn*
adder	la vipère	*lah veepehr*
addition	l'addition (f.)	*lahdeesyawn*
address	l'adresse (f.)	*lahdrehs*
admission	l'entrée (f.)	*lohntray*
admission price	le prix d'entrée	*luh pree dohntray*
advice	le conseil	*luh kawnsehy*
after	après	*ahpreh*
afternoon	l'après-midi (m., f.)	*lahpreh meedee*
aftershave	la lotion après-rasage	*lah loasyawn*
		ahpreh rahzahjh
again	à nouveau	*ah noovoa*
against	contre	*kawntr*
age	l'âge (m.)	*lahjh*
Aids	le sida	*luh seedah*
air conditioning	l'air conditionné (m.)	*lehr kawndeesyonay*
air mattress	le matelas	*luh mahtlah*
	pneumatique	*pnuhmahteek*
air sickness bag	le petit sac à	*luh puhtee sahk ah*
	vomissements	*vomeesmohn*
aircraft	l'avion (m.)	*lahvyawn*
airport	l'aéroport (m.)	*lahayroapor*
alarm	l'alarme (f.)	*lahlahrm*
alarm clock	le réveil	*luh rayvehy*
alcohol	l'alcool (m.)	*lahlkol*
A-level equivalent	le bac	*luh bahk*
a little	un peu	*uhn puh*
allergic	allergique	*ahlehrjheek*
alone	seul	*suhl*
always	toujours	*toojhoor*
ambulance	l'ambulance (f.)	*lohnbewlohns*
amount	le montant	*luh mawntohn*
amusement park	le parc d'attractions	*luh pahrk*
		dahtrahksyawn
anaesthetize	anesthésier	*ahnehstayzyay*
anchovy	l'anchois (m.)	*lohnshwah*
and	et	*ay*
angry	en colère	*ohn kolehr*
animal	l'animal (m.)	*lahneemahl*
answer	la réponse	*lah raypawns*
ant	la fourmi	*lah foormee*

antibiotics	l'antibiotique (m.)	*lohnteebyoteek*
antifreeze	l'antigel (m.)	*lohnteejhehl*
antique	ancien	*ohnsyahn*
antiques	antiquités (f.)	*ohnteekeetay*
anus	l'anus (m.)	*lahnews*
apartment	l'appartement (m.)	*lahpahrtuhmohn*
aperitif	l'apéritif (m.)	*lahpayroctoef*
apologies	les excuses	*lay zehxkewz*
apple	la pomme	*lah pom*
apple juice	le jus de pommes	*luh jhew duh pom*
apple pie	la tarte aux pommes	*lah tahrt oa pom*
apple sauce	la compote de	*lah kawnpot*
	pommes	*duh pom*
appointment	le rendez-vous	*luh rohndayvoo*
apricot	l'abricot (m.)	*lahbreekoa*
April	avril	*ahvreel*
archbishop	l'archevèque (m.)	*lahrshuhvehk*
architecture	l'architecture (f.)	*lahrsheetehktewr*
area	les environs	*lay zohnveerawn*
arm	le bras	*luh brah*
arrive	arriver	*ahreevay*
arrow	la flèche	*lah flehsh*
art	l'art (m.)	*lahr*
artery	l'artère (f.)	*lahrtehr*
artichoke	l'artichaut (m.)	*lahrteeshoa*
article	l'article (m.)	*lahrteekl*
artificial respiration	la respiration	*lah rehspeerahsyawn*
	artificielle	*ahrteefeesyehl*
arts and crafts	l'artisanat d'art	*lahrteezahnah dahr*
ashtray	le cendrier	*luh sohndreeay*
ask	demander	*duhmohnday*
ask	prier	*preeay*
asparagus	les asperges	*lay zahspehrjh*
aspirin	l'aspirine (f.)	*lahspeereen*
assault	l'agression (f.)	*lahgrehsyawn*
at home	à la maison	*ah lah mehzawn*
at night	la nuit	*lah nwee*
at the back	à l'arrière	*ah lahryehr*
at the front	à l'avant	*ah lahvohn*
at the latest	au plus tard	*oa plew tahr*
aubergine	l'aubergine (f.)	*loabehrjheen*
August	aôut	*oot*
automatic	automatique	*loatoamahteek*
automatically	automatiquement	*oatoamahteekmohn*
autumn	l'automne (m.)	*loatonn*
avalanche	l'avalanche (f.)	*lahvahlohnsh*
awake	réveillé	*rayvay-yay*
awning	le parasol	*luh pahrahsol*

B

baby	le bébé	*luh baybay*
baby food	la nourriture pour	*lah nooreetewr poor*
	bébé	*baybay*
babysitter	le/la baby-sitter	*luh/lah behbee seetehr*
back	le dos	*luh doa*
backpack	le sac à dos	*luh sahk ah doa*

bacon	le lard	*luh lahr*
bad	mauvais	*moaveh*
bag	le sac	*luh sahk*
baker (cakes)	le pâtissier	*luh pahteesyay*
baker	le boulanger	*luh boolohnjhay*
balcony (theatre)	le balcon	*luh bahlkawn*
balcony (to building)	le balcon	*luh bahlkawn*
ball	la balle	*lah bahl*
ballet	le ballet; la danse	*luh bahleh; la dohns*
ballpoint pen	le stylo à bille	*luh steeloa ah beey*
banana	la banane	*lah bahnahn*
bandage	le pansement	*luh pohnsmohn*
bank (river)	la rive	*lah reev*
bank	la banque	*lah bohnk*
bank card	la carte bancaire	*lah kahrt bohnkehr*
bar (café)	le bar	*luh bahr*
bar (drinks' cabinet)	le bar	*luh bahr*
barbecue	le barbecue	*luh bahrbuhkew*
bath	le bain	*luh bahn*
bath attendant	le maître nageur	*luh mehtr nahjhuhr*
bath foam	la mousse de bain	*lah moos duh bahn*
bath towel	la serviette de bain	*lah sehrvyeht duh bahn*
bathing cap	le bonnet de bain	*luh boneh duh bahn*
bathing cubicle	la cabine de bain	*lah kahbeen duh bahn*
bathing suit	le maillot de bain	*luh mahyoa duh bahn*
bathroom	la salle de bain	*lah sahl duh bahn*
battery (car)	l'accumulateur (m.)	*lahkewmewlahtuhr*
battery	la pile	*lah peel*
beach	la plage	*lah plahjh*
beans	les haricots	*lay ahreekoa*
beautiful	beau/belle	*boa/behl*
beautiful	magnifique	*mahnyeefook*
beauty parlour	le salon de beauté	*luh sahlawn duh boatay*
bed	le lit	*luh lee*
bee	l'abeille (f.)	*lahbehy*
beef	la viande de boeuf	*lah vyohnd duh buhf*
beer	la bière	*lah byehr*
beetroot	la betterave	*lah behtrahv*
begin	commencer	*komohnsay*
beginner	le débutant	*luh daybewtohn*
behind	derrière	*dehryehr*
Belgian (f)	la belge	*lah behljh*
Belgian (m)	le belge	*luh behljh*
Belgium	la Belgique	*lah behljheek*
belt	la ceinture	*lah sahntewr*
berth	la couchette	*lah koosheht*
better	mieux	*myuh*
bicarbonate of soda	le bicarbonate de soude	*luh beekahrbonaht duh sood*
bicycle	la bicyclette/le vélo	*lah beeseekleht/luh vayloa*
bicycle pump	la pompe à bicyclette	*lah pawnp ah beeseekleht*
bicycle repairman	le réparateur de vélos	*luh raypahrahtuhr duh vayloa*
bikini	le bikini	*luh beekeenee*
bill	l'addition	*lahdeesyawn*

birthday	l'anniversaire (m.)	lahneevehrsehr
biscuit	le biscuit	luh beeskwee
bite	mordre	mordr
bitter	amer	ahmehr
black	noir	nwahr
bland	fade	fahd
blanket	la couverture	lah koovehrtewr
bleach	blondir	blawndeer
blister	la cloque	lah klok
blond	blond	blawn
blood	le sang	luh sohn
blood pressure	la tension	lah tohnsyawn
blouse	le chemisier	luh shuhmeezyay
blow dry	sécher	sayshay
blue	bleu	bluh
blunt	épointé/émoussé	aypwahntay/aymoosay
boat	le bateau	luh bahtoa
body	le corps	luh kor
body milk	le lait corporel	luh leh korporehl
boil	bouillir	boo-yeer
boiled	cuit	kwee
boiled ham	jambon cuit	jhohnbawn kwee
bone	l'os (m.)	los
bonnet	le capot	luh kahpoa
book (verb)	réserver	raysehrvay
book	le livre	luh leevr
booked	réservé	rayzehrvay
booking office	le bureau de réservation	luh bewroa duh rayzehrvahsyawn
bookshop	la librairie	lah leebrehree
border	la frontière	lah frawntyehr
bored (to be)	s'ennuyer	sonweeyay
boring	ennuyeux	onweeyuh
born	né	nay
botanical gardens	le jardin botanique	luh jhahrdahn botahneek
both	tous/toutes les deux	too/toot lay duh
bottle-warmer	le chauffe-biberon	luh shoaf beebrawn
bottle (baby's)	le biberon	luh beebrawn
bottle	la bouteille	lah bootehy
box	la boîte	lah bwaht
box (theatre)	la loge	lah lojh
boy	le garçon	luh gahrsawn
bra	le soutien-gorge	luh sootyahn gorjh
bracelet	le bracelet	luh brahsleh
braised	braisé	brehzay
brake	le frein	luh frahn
brake fluid	le liquide de freins	luh leekeed duh frahn
brake oil	l'huile à frein (f.)	lweel ah frahn
bread	le pain	luh pahn
break	casser	kahssay
breakfast	le petit déjeuner	luh puhtee dayjhuhnay
breast	la poitrine	lah pwahtreen
bridge	le pont	luh pawn
briefs	la culotte	lah kewlot
brochure	la brochure	lah broshewr
broken	cassé	kahssay

broth	le consommé	*luh kawnsomay*
brother	le frère	*luh frehr*
brown	brun	*bruhn*
brush	la brosse	*lah bros*
Brussels sprouts	les choux de Bruxelles	*lay shoo duh brewxehl*
bucket	le seau	*luh soa*
bugs	les insectes nuisibles	*lay zahnsehkt nweezeebl*
building	le bâtiment	*luh bahteemohn*
buoy	la bouée	*lah booway*
burglary	le cambriolage	*luh kohnbryolajh*
burn (verb)	brûler	*brewlay*
burn	la brûlure	*lah brewlewr*
burnt	brûlé	*brewlay*
bus	l'autobus (m.)	*loatoabews*
bus station	la station d'autobus	*lah stahsyawn doatoabews*
bus stop	l'arrêt d'autobus (m.)	*lahreh doatoabews*
business class	la classe affaire (f.)	*lah klahs ahfehr*
business trip	le voyage d'affaires	*luh vwahyahjh dahfehr*
busy	animé	*ahneemay*
butane gas	le gaz butane	*luh gahz bewtahnn*
butcher	le boucher	*luh booshay*
butter	le beurre	*luh buhr*
button	le bouton	*luh bootawn*
buy	acheter	*ahshtay*
by airmail	la poste aérienne/ par avion	*lah post ahayryehn/ pahr ahvyawn*

C

cabbage	le chou	*luh shoo*
cabin	la cabine	*lah kahbeen*
cake	le gâteau	*luh gahtoa*
call	appeler	*ahpuhlay*
called (to be)	s'appeler	*sahpuhlay*
camera	l'appareil-photo (m.)	*lahpahrehy foatoa*
camp	faire du camping	*fehr dew kohnpeeng*
camp shop	le magasin du camping	*luh mahgahzahn dew kohnpeeng*
camp site	le camping	*luh kohnpeeng*
camper	le camping-car	*luh kohnpeeng kahr*
campfire	le feu de camp	*luh fuh duh kohn*
camping guide	le guide de camping	*luh gueed duh kohnpeeng*
camping permit	le permis de camping	*luh pehrmee duh kohnpeeng*
canal boat	la péniche	*lah payneesh*
cancel	annuler	*ahnewlay*
candle	la bougie	*lah boojhee*
canoe (verb)	faire du canoë	*fehr dew kahnoaeh*
canoe	le canoë	*luh kahnoaeh*
car (train)	le wagon	*luh vahgawn*
car	la voiture	*lah vwahtewr*
car deck	le pont à voitures	*luh pawn ah vwahtewr*
car documents	les papiers de voiture	*lay pahpyay duh vwahtewr*

car trouble	la panne	*lah pahnn*
carafe	la carafe	*lah kahrahf*
caravan	la caravane	*lah kahrahvahnn*
cardigan	le cardigan/le gilet	*luh kahrdeegahn/ luh jheeleh*
careful	prudent	*prewdohn*
carrot	la carotte	*lah kahrot*
cartridge	la cartouche	*lah kahrtoosh*
cartridge	la cassette	*lah kahseht*
cascade	la cascade	*lah kahskahd*
cash desk	la caisse	*lah kehss*
casino	le casino	*luh kahzeenoa*
cassette	la cassette	*lah kahseht*
castle	le château	*luh shahtoa*
cat	le chat	*luh shah*
catalogue	le catalogue	*luh kahtahlog*
cathedral	la cathédrale	*lah kahtaydrahl*
cauliflower	le chou-fleur	*luh shoo fluhr*
cave	la grotte	*lah grot*
CD	le compact disc	*luh kawnpahkt deesk*
celebrate	célébrer	*saylaybray*
cellotape	le scotch	*luh skoch*
cemetery	le cimetière	*luh seemtyehr*
centimetre	le centimètre	*luh sohnteemehtr*
central heating	le chauffage central	*luh shoafahjh sohntrahl*
centre (in the)	au milieu	*oa meelyuh*
centre	le centre	*luh sohntr*
cereal	la céréale	*lah sayrayahl*
chair	la chaise	*lah shehz*
chambermaid	la femme de chambre	*lah fahm duh shohnbr*
chamois	la peau de chamois	*lah poa duh shahmwah*
champagne	le champagne	*luh shohnpany*
change (verb)	modifier	*modeefyay*
	changer	*shohnjhay*
change	la monnaie	*lah moneh*
change the baby's nappy	changer la couche du bébé	*shohnjhay lah koosh dew baybay*
change the oil	changer l'huile	*shohnjhay lweel*
chapel	la chapelle	*lah shahpehl*
charcoal tablets	les pastilles de charbon	*lay pahsteey duh shahrbawn*
charter flight	le vol charter	*luh vol shahrtehr*
chat up	draguer	*drahgay*
check (verb)	contrôler	*kawntroalay*
check in	enregistrer	*ohnruhjheestray*
cheers	à votre santé	*ah votr sohntay*
cheese	le fromage	*luh fromahjh*
chef	le chef	*luh shehf*
chemist	la pharmacie	*lah fahrmahsee*
cheque	le chèque	*luh shehk*
cherries	les cerises	*lay suhreez*
chess (play)	jouer aux échecs	*jhooay oa zayshehk*
chewing gum	le chewing-gum	*luh shweenguhm*
chicken	le poulet	*luh pooleh*
chicory	les endives	*lay zohndeev*
child	l'enfant (m./f.)	*lohnfohn*
child seat	le siège-enfant	*luh seeyehjh ohnfohn*

chilled	rafraîchi	*rahfrehshee*
chin	le menton	*luh montawn*
chips	les pommes-frites	*lay pom freet*
chocolate	le chocolat	*luh shoakoalah*
choose	choisir	*shwahzeer*
chop	la côtelette	*lah koatuhleht*
christian name	le prénom	*luh praynawn*
church	l'église (f.)	*laygleez*
church service	le service religieux	*luh sehrvees ruhleejhyuh*
cigar	le cigare	*luh seegahr*
cigar shop	le tabac	*luh tahbah*
cigarette	la cigarette	*lah seegahreht*
cigarette paper	le papier à cigarettes	*luh pahpyay ah seegahreht*
cine camera	la caméra	*lah kahmayrah*
circle	le cercle	*luh sehrkl*
circus	le cirque	*luh seerk*
city	la ville	*lah veel*
map	le plan	*luh plohn*
classical concert	le concert classique	*luh kawnsehr klahsseek*
clean (verb)	nettoyer	*nehtwahyay*
clean	propre	*propr*
clear	clair	*klehr*
clearance	les soldes	*lay sold*
closed	fermé	*fehrmay*
closed off	bloqué	*blokay*
clothes	les habits	*lay zahbee*
clothes hanger	le cintre	*luh sahntr*
clothes peg	la pince à linge	*lah pahns ah lahnjh*
clothing	vêtements	*vehtmohn*
coach	l'autobus (m.)	*loatoabews*
coat	le manteau	*luh mohntoa*
cockroach	le cafard	*luh kahfahr*
cocoa	le cacao	*luh kahkahoa*
cod	le cabillaud	*luh kahbeeyoa*
coffee	le café	*luh kahfay*
coffee filter	le filtre de cafetière	*luh feeltr duh kahftyehr*
cognac	le cognac	*luh konyahk*
cold	froid	*frwah*
cold	le rhume	*luh rewm*
cold cuts	la charcuterie	*lah shahrkewtree*
collarbone	la clavicule	*lah klahveekewl*
colleague	le collègue	*luh kolehg*
collision	la collision	*lah koleezyawn*
cologne	l'eau de toilette (f.)	*loa duh twahleht*
colour	la couleur	*lah kooluhr*
colour pencils	les crayons de couleur	*lay krayawn duh kooluhr*
colour TV	la télévision en couleurs	*lah taylayveezyawn ohn kooluhr*
colouring book	l'album de coloriage (m.)	*lahlbuhm duh koloryajh*
comb	le peigne	*luh pehnyuh*
come	venir	*vuhneer*
come back	revenir	*ruhvuhneer*

compartment	le compartiment	*luh kawnpahrteemohn*
complaint	la plainte	*lah plahnt*
complaints book	le cahier de réclamations	*luh kahyay duh rayklahmahsyawn*
completely	entièrement	*ohntyehrmohn*
compliment	le compliment	*luh kawnpleemohn*
compulsory	obligatoire	*obleegahtwahr*
concert	le concert	*luh kawnsehr*
concert hall	la salle de concert	*lah sahl duh kawnsehr*
concussion	la commotion cérébrale	*lah koamoasyawn sayraybrahl*
condensed milk	le lait condensé	*luh leh kawndohnsay*
condom	le préservatif	*luh prayzehrvahteef*
congratulate	féliciter	*fayleeseetay*
connection	la liaison	*lah lyehzawn*
constipation	la constipation	*lah kawnsteepahsyawn*
consulate	le consulat	*luh kownsewlah*
consultation	la consultation	*lah kawnsewltahsyawn*
contact lens	la lentille de contact	*lah lohnteey duh kawntahkt*
contact lens solution	le liquide pour lentille de contact	*luh leekeed poor lohnteey duh kawntahkt*
contagious	contagieux	*kawntahjhyuh*
contraceptive	le contraceptif	*luh kawntrahsehpteef*
contraceptive pill	la pilule anticonceptionnelle	*lah peelewl ohnteekawnsehpsyonehl*
convent	le couvent	*luh koovohn*
cook (verb)	cuisiner	*kweezeenay*
cook	le cuisinier	*luh kweezeenyay*
copper	le cuivre	*luh kweevr*
copy	la copie	*lah kopee*
corkscrew	le tire-bouchon	*luh teerbooshawn*
cornflour	la maïzena	*lah maheezaynah*
corner	le coin	*luh kwahn*
correct	correct	*korehkt*
correspond	correspondre	*korehspawndr*
corridor	le couloir	*luh koolwahr*
costume	le costume	*luh kostewm*
cot	le lit d'enfant	*luh lee dohnfohn*
cotton	le coton	*luh koatawn*
cotton wool	le coton	*luh koatawn*
cough	la toux	*lah too*
cough mixture	le sirop pectoral	*luh seeroa pehktoaral*
counter	la réception	*lah raysehpsyawn*
country	le pays	*luh pehy*
country	la campagne	*lah kohnpahnyuh*
country code	l'indicatif du pays (m.)	*lahndeekahteef dew pehy*
courgette	la courgette	*lah koorjheht*
cousin (f)	la cousine	*lah koozeen*
cousin (m)	le cousin	*luh koozahn*
crab	le crabe	*luh krahb*
cream	la crème	*lah krehm*

credit card	la carte de crédit	*lah kahrt duh kraydee*
crisps	les chips	*lay sheeps*
croissant	le croissant	*luh krwahssohn*
cross-country run	la piste de ski de fond	*lah peest duh skee duh fawn*
cross-country skiing	faire du ski de fond	*fehr dew skee duh fawn*
cross-country skis	les skis de fond	*lay skee duh fawn*
cross the road	traverser	*trahvehrsay*
crossing	la traversée	*lah trahvehrsay*
crossing	le croisement	*luh krwahzmohn*
cry	pleurer	*pluhray*
cubic metre	le mètre cube	*luh mehtr kewb*
cucumber	le concombre	*luh kawnkawnbr*
cuddly toy	l'animal en peluche (m.)	*lahneemahl ohn plewsh*
cuff links	les boutons de manchette	*lay bootawn duh mohnsheht*
cup	la tasse	*lah tahs*
curly	frisé	*freezay*
current	la circulation	*lah seerkewlahsyawn*
cushion	le coussin	*luh koossahn*
customary	habituel	*ahbeetewehl*
customs	la douane	*lah dwahnn*
customs	le contrôle douanier	*luh kawntrol dwahnnyay*
cut (verb)	couper	*koopay*
cutlery	couverts	*koovehr*
cycling	faire de la bicyclette/ du vélo	*fehr duh lah beeseekleht/dew vayloa*

D

dairy produce	les produits laitiers	*lay prodwcc laytyay*
damaged	abîmé	*ahbeemay*
dance	danser	*dohnsay*
dandruff	les pellicules	*lay payleekewl*
danger	le danger	*luh dohnjhay*
dangerous	dangereux	*dohnjhuhruh*
dark	sombre	*sawnbr*
date	le rendez-vous	*luh rohndayvoo*
daughter	la fille	*lah feey*
day	le jour	*luh jhoor*
day after tomorrow	après-demain	*ahpreh duhmahn*
day before yesterday	avant-hier	*ahvohn tyehr*
death	la mort	*lah mor*
decaffeinated	le décaféiné	*luh daykahfayeenay*
December	décembre	*daysohnbr*
deck chair	la chaise longue	*lah shehz lawng*
declare(customs)	déclarer	*dayklahray*
deep	profond	*profawn*
deep sea diving	la plongée sous-marine	*lah plawnjhay soo mahreen*
deepfreeze	le congélateur	*luh kawnjhaylahtuhr*
degrees	les degrés	*lay duhgray*
delay	le retard	*luh ruhtahr*
delicious	délicieux	*dayleesyuh*

dentist	le dentiste	*luh dohnteest*
dentures	le dentier	*luh dohntyay*
deodorant	le déodorant	*luh dayodorohn*
department	le rayon	*luh rayawn*
department store	le grand magasin	*luh grohn mahgahzahn*
departure	le départ	*luh daypahr*
departure time	l'heure de départ (f.)	*ler duh daypahr*
depilatory cream	la crème épilatoire	*lah krehm aypeelahtwahr*
deposit	arrhes, acompte	*ahr, ahkawnt*
dessert	le dessert	*luh dehssehr*
destination	la destination	*lah dehsteenahsyawn*
develop	développer	*dayvlopay*
diabetes	le diabète	*luh deeahbeht*
diabetic	le diabétique	*luh dyahbayteek*
dial	composer	*kawnpoazay*
diamond	le diamant	*luh deeahmohn*
diarrhoea	la diarrhée	*lah deeahray*
dictionary	le dictionnaire	*luh deeksyonehr*
diesel	le diesel	*luh dyayzehl*
diesel oil	le gas-oil	*luh gahzwahl*
diet	le régime	*luh rayjheem*
difficulty	la difficulté	*lah deefeekewltay*
dining room	la salle à manger	*lah sahl ah mohnjhay*
dining/buffet car	le wagon-restaurant	*luh vahgawn rehstoaron*
dinner (to have)	dîner	*deenay*
dinner	le dîner	*luh deenay*
dinner jacket	le smoking	*luh smokeeng*
direction	la direction	*lah deerehksyawn*
directly	directement	*deerehktuhmohn*
dirty	sale	*sahl*
disabled	l'invalide (m./f.)	*lahnvahleed*
disco	la discothèque	*lah deeskotehk*
discount	la réduction	*lah raydewksyawn*
disgusting	dégoûtant	*daygootohn*
dish	le plat	*luh plah*
dish of the day	le plat du jour	*luh plah dew jhoor*
disinfectant	le désinfectant	*luh dayzahnfehktohn*
distance	la distance	*lah deestohns*
distilled water	l'eau distillée (f.)	*loa deesteelay*
disturb	déranger	*dayrohnjhay*
disturbance	troubles, tapage	*troobl, tapahjh*
dive	plonger	*plawnjhay*
diving	la plongée	*lah plawnjhay*
diving board	le plongeoir	*luh plawnjhwahr*
diving gear	l'équipement de plongeur (m.)	*laykeepmohn duh plawnjhuhr*
DIY-shop	le magasin de bricolage	*luh mahgahzahn duh breekolajh*
dizzy	pris de vertige	*pree duh vehrteejh*
do (verb)	faire	*fehr*
doctor	le médecin	*luh maydsahn*
dog	le chien	*luh shyahn*
doll	la poupée	*lah poopay*

domestic	l'intérieur (m.)	*lahntayryuhr*
	du pays	*dew pehy*
door	la porte	*lah port*
down	en bas	*ohn bah*
draught	le courant d'air	*luh koorohn dehr*
dream	rêver	*rehvay*
dress	la robe	*lah rob*
dressing gown	le peignoir	*luh paynywahr*
drink (verb)	boire	*bwahr*
drink	le verre	*luh vehr*
drinking chocolate	le chocolat au lait	*luh shoakoalah oa leh*
drinking water	l'eau potable (f.)	*loa potabl*
drive	conduire	*kawndweer*
driver	le chauffeur	*luh shoafuhr*
driving licence	le permis de	*luh pehrmee duh*
	conduire	*kawndweer*
drought	la sécheresse	*lah sayshrehs*
dry (verb)	sécher	*sayshay*
dry	sec	*sehk*
dry clean	nettoyer à sec	*nehtwahyay ah sehk*
dry cleaner's	la teinturerie	*lah tahntewruhree*
dry shampoo	le shampooing sec	*luh shohnpwahn sehk*
dummy	la tétine	*lah tayteen*
during	pendant	*pohndohn*
during the day	de jour	*duh jhoor*

E

each time	chaque fois	*shahk fwah*
ear	l'oreille (f.)	*lorehy*
ear, nose and throat (ENT) specialist	l'oto-rhino (m.)	*loatoa reenoa*
earache	le mal d'oreille	*luh mahl dorehy*
eardrops	les gouttes pour	*lay goot poor*
	les oreilles	*lay zorehy*
early	tôt	*toa*
earrings	les boucles d'oreilles	*lay bookl dorehy*
earth	la terre	*lah tehr*
earthenware	la poterie	*lah potree*
east	l'est (m.)	*lehst*
easy	facile	*fahseel*
eat	manger	*mohnjhay*
eczema	l'eczéma (m.)	*lehgzaymah*
eel	l'anguille (f.)	*lohngeey*
egg	l'oeuf (m.)	*luhf*
elastic band	l'élastique (m.)	*laylahsteek*
electric	électrique	*aylehktreek*
electric current	le courant	*luh koorohn*
electricity	l'électricité (f.)	*laylehktreeseetay*
embassy	l'ambassade (f.)	*lohnbahsahd*
emergency brake	le frein de secours	*luh frahn duh suhkoor*
emergency exit	la sortie de secours	*lah sortee duh suhkoor*
emergency number	le numéro	*luh newmayroa*
	d'urgence (m.)	*dewrzhohns*
emergency phone	le téléphone	*luh taylayfon*
	d'urgence (m.)	*dewrjhohns*
emergency triangle	le triangle de	*luh treeohngl duh*
	signalisation	*seenyahleezahsyawn*

Word list

15

emery board	la lime à ongles	lah leem ah awngl
empty	vide	veed
engaged	occupé	okewpay
England	Angleterre	ohngluhtehr
English	anglais	ohngleh
entertainment guide	le journal des spectacles	luh jhoornal day spehktahkl
envelope	l'enveloppe (f.)	lohnvlop
escort	l'hôtesse	loatehs
evening	le soir	luh swahr
evening wear	la tenue de soirée	lah tuhnew duh swahray
event	l'évènement (m.)	layvehnmohn
everything	tout	too
everywhere	partout	pahrtoo
examine	examiner	ehgzahmeenay
excavation	les fouilles	lay fooeey
excellent	excellent	ehxaylohn
exchange	échanger	ayshohnjhay
exchange office	le bureau de change	luh bewroa duh shohnjh
exchange rate	le cours du change	luh koor dew shohnjh
excursion	l'excursion (f.)	lehxkewrsyawn
exhibition	l'exposition (f.)	lehxpoazeesyawn
exit	la sortie	lah sortee
expenses	les frais	lay freh
expensive	cher	shehr
explain	expliquer	ehxpleekay
express	l'express (m.)	lehxprehs
external	extérieur	ehxtayryuhr
eye	l'oeil (m.)	luhy
eye drops	les gouttes pour les yeux	lay goot poor lay zyuh
eye shadow	le fard à paupières	luh fahr ah poapyehr
eye specialist	l'ophtalmologue (m.)	loftahmolog
eyeliner	l'eye-liner (m.)	lahy leehnehr

F

face	le visage	luh veezajh
factory	l'usine (f.)	lewzeen
fair	la foire	lah fwahr
fall	tomber	tawnbay
family	la famille	lah fahmeey
famous	célèbre	saylehbr
far away	éloigné	aylwahnyay
farm	la ferme	lah fehrm
farmer	le fermier	luh fehrmyay
fashion	la mode	lah mod
fast	rapidement	rahpeedmohn
father	le père	luh pehr
fault	la faute	lah foat
fax	faxer	fahxay
fear	la peur	lah puhr
February	février	fayvryay
feel	sentir	sohnteer
feel like	avoir envie (de)	ahvwahr ohnvee (duh)
fence	la clôture	lah kloatewr

fever	la fièvre	*lah feeyehvr*
fill (tooth)	plomber	*plawnbay*
fill out	remplir	*rohnpleer*
filling	le plombage	*luh plawnbahjh*
film	la pellicule	*lah payleekewl*
filter	le filtre	*luh feeltr*
filthy	crasseux	*krahssuh*
find	trouver	*troovay*
fine	la caution	*lah koasyawn*
fine (parking)	la contravention	*lah kawntrahvohn-syawn*
finger	le doigt	*luh dwah*
fire	le feu	*luh fuh*
fire brigade	les sapeurs-pompiers	*lay sahpuhr pawnpay*
fire escape	l'escalier de secours (m.)	*lehskahlyay duh suhkoor*
fire extinguisher	l'extincteur (m.)	*lehxtahntuhr*
first	le premier	*luh pruhmyay*
first aid	les premiers soins	*lay pruhmyay swahn*
first class	la première classe	*lah pruhmyehr klahs*
fish (verb)	pêcher	*payshay*
fish	le poisson	*luh pwahssawn*
fishing rod	la canne à pêche	*lah kahnn ah pehsh*
fitness centre	le centre de mise en forme	*luh sohntr duh meez ohn form*
fitness training	l'entraînement de mise en forme (m.)	*lohntrehnmohn duh meez ohn form*
fitting room	la cabine d'essayage	*lah kahbeen dehsayahjh*
fix	réparer	*raypahray*
flag	le drapeau	*luh drahpoa*
flash bulb	l'ampoule de flash (f.)	*lohnpool duh flahsh*
flash cube	le cube-flash	*luh kewb flahsh*
flash gun	le flash	*luh flahsh*
flat	l'appartement (m.)	*lahpahrtuhmohn*
flea market	le marché aux puces	*luh mahrshay oa pews*
flight	le vol	*luh vol*
flight number	le numéro de vol	*luh newmayroa duh vol*
flood	l'inondation (f.)	*leenawndahsyawn*
floor	l'étage (m.)	*laytahjh*
flour	la farine	*lah fahreen*
flu	la grippe	*lah greep*
fly-over	l'autopont (m.)	*loatoapawn*
fly (insect)	la mouche	*lah moosh*
fly (verb)	voler	*volay*
fog	le brouillard	*luh brooy-yahr*
foggy (to be)	faire du brouillard	*fehr dew brooy-yahr*
folding caravan	la caravane pliante	*lah kahrahvahnn pleeohnt*
folkloristic	folklorique	*folkloreek*
follow	suivre	*sweevr*
food	la nourriture	*lah nooreetewr*
food poisoning	l'intoxication alimentaire (f.)	*lahntoxeekahsyawn ahleemohntehr*
foodstuffs	les produits alimentaires	*lay prohdwee zahleemohntehr*
foot	le pied	*luh pyay*

Word list

15

for hire	à louer	*ah looay*
forbidden	interdit	*ahntehrdee*
forehead	le front	*luh frawn*
foreign	étranger	*aytrohnjhay*
forget	oublier	*oobleeay*
fork	la fourchette	*lah foorsheht*
form	le questionnaire	*luh kehstyonehr*
fort	le fort	*luh for*
fountain	la fontaine	*lah fawntehn*
four star petrol	le super	*luh sewpehr*
frame	la monture	*lah mawntewr*
franc	le franc	*luh frohn*
free	libre	*leebr*
free of charge	gratuit	*grahtwee*
free time	les loisirs	*lay lwahzeer*
freeze	geler	*jhuhlay*
French	français	*frohnseh*
French (language)	le français	*luh frohnseh*
French bread	la baguette	*lah bahgeht*
fresh	frais	*freh*
Friday	vendredi	*vohndruhdee*
fried	frit	*free*
fried egg	l'oeuf sur le plat (m.)	*luhf sewr luh plah*
friend	l'ami(e) (m./f.)	*lahmee*
friendly	amical	*ahmeekahl*
fringe	la frange	*lah frohnjh*
fruit	le fruit	*luh frwee*
fruit juice	le jus de fruits	*luh jhew duh frwee*
frying pan	la poêle à frire	*lah pwahl ah freer*
full	plein	*plahn*
fun	le plaisir	*luh playzeer*
funny	drôle	*droal*

G

gallery	la galerie	*lah gahlree*
game	le jeu	*luh jhuh*
garage	le garage	*luh gahrahjh*
garbage bag	le sac poubelle	*luh sahk poobehl*
garden	le jardin	*luh jhahrdahn*
gastroenteritis	la gastro-entérite	*gahstroa ohntayreet*
gauze	la compresse de gaze	*lah kawnprehs duh gahz*
gel	le gel	*luh jhehl*
German	allemand	*ahlmohn*
get married	(se) marier	*(suh) mahryay*
get off	descendre	*daysohndr*
gift	le cadeau	*luh kahdoa*
gilt	doré	*doray*
ginger	le gingembre	*luh jhahnjhohnbr*
girl	la fille	*lah feey*
girlfriend	l'amie	*lahmee*
giro card	la carte de chèque postal	*lah kahrt duh shehk postahl*
giro cheque	le chèque postal	*luh shehk postahl*
glacier	le glacier	*luh glahsyay*
glass (wine -)	le verre	*luh vehr*
glasses (sun -)	les lunettes	*lay lewneht*

glide	faire du vol à voile	*fehr dew vol ah vwahl*
glove	le gant	*luh gohn*
glue	la colle	*lah kol*
go	aller	*ahlay*
go back	reculer, retourner	*ruhkewlay, ruhtoornay*
go out	sortir	*sorteer*
goat's cheese	le fromage de chèvre	*luh fromajh duh shehvr*
gold	l'or (m.)	*lor*
golf course	le terrain de golf	*luh tehrahn duh golf*
good afternoon	bonjour	*bawnjhoor*
good evening	bonsoir	*bawnswahr*
good morning	bonjour	*bawnjhoor*
good night	bonne nuit	*bon nwee*
goodbye	au revoir	*oa ruhvwahr*
gram	le gramme	*luh grahm*
grandchild	le petit enfant	*luh puhtee tohnfohn*
grandfather	le grand-père	*luh grohn pehr*
grandmother	la grand-mère	*lah grohn mehr*
grape juice	le jus de raisin	*luh jhew duh rayzahn*
grapefruit	le pamplemousse	*luh pohnpluhmoos*
grapes	les raisins	*lay rayzahn*
grass	l'herbe (f.)	*lehrb*
grave	la tombe	*lah townb*
greasy	gras	*grah*
green	vert	*vehr*
green card	la carte verte	*lah kahrt vehrt*
greet	saluer	*sahleway*
grey	gris	*gree*
grill	griller	*greeyay*
grilled	grillé	*greeyay*
grocer	l'épicier (m)	*laypeesyay*
ground	le sol	*luh sol*
group	le groupe	*luh groop*
guest house	la pension	*lah pohnsyawn*
guide (book)	le guide	*luh gueed*
guide (person)	le/la guide	*luh/lah gueed*
guided tour	la visite guidée	*lah veezeet gueeday*
gynaecologist	le gynécologue	*luh jheenaykolog*

H

hair	les cheveux	*lay shuhvuh*
hairbrush	la brosse à cheveux	*lah bros ah shuhvuh*
hairdresser	le coiffeur	*luh kwahfuhr*
hairslides	les barrettes	*lay bahreht*
hairspray	la laque	*lah lahk*
half (adj.)	demi	*duhmee*
half	la moitié	*lah mwahtyay*
half full	à moitié plein	*ah mwahtyay plahn*
hammer	le marteau	*luh mahrtoa*
hand	la main	*lah mahn*
hand brake	le frein à main	*luh frahn ah mahn*
handbag	le sac à main	*luh sahk ah mahn*
handkerchief	le mouchoir	*luh mooshwahr*
handmade	fait-main	*feh mahn*
happy	heureux	*uhruh*
harbour	le port	*luh por*
hard	dur	*dewr*

hat	le chapeau	*luh shahpoa*
hay fever	le rhume des foins	*luh rewm day fwahn*
hazelnut	la noisette	*lah nwahzeht*
head	la tête	*lah teht*
headache	le mal de tête	*luh mahl duh teht*
headscarf	le foulard	*luh foolahr*
health	la santé	*lah sohntay*
health food shop	le magasin	*luh mahgahzahn*
	diététique	*dyaytayteek*
hear	entendre	*ohntohndr*
hearing aid	la correction	*lah korehksyawn*
	auditive	*oadeeteev*
heart	le coeur	*luh kuhr*
heater	le chauffage	*luh shoafahjh*
heavy	lourd	*loor*
heel	le talon	*luh tahlawn*
hello	bonjour, salut	*bawnjhoor, sahlew*
helmet	le casque	*luh kahsk*
help (verb)	aider	*ayday*
help	l'aide (f.)	*lehd*
herbal tea	l'infusion (f.)	*lahnfewzyawn*
here	ici	*eesee*
herring	le hareng	*luh ahrohn*
high	haut	*oa*
high tide	le flux	*luh flew*
highchair	la chaise d'enfant	*lah shehz dohnfohn*
hiking	la marche à pied	*lah mahrsh ah pyay*
hiking trip	la randonnée	*lah rohndonay*
hip	la hanche	*lah ohnsh*
hire	louer	*looay*
hitchhike	faire de l'auto-stop	*fehr duh loatoastop*
hobby	le passe-temps	*luh pahstohn*
hold-up	l'attaque (f.)	*lahtahk*
holiday house	la maison de	*lah mehzawn duh*
	vacances	*vahkohns*
holidays	les vacances	*lay vahkohns*
homesickness	le mal du pays	*luh mahl dew pehy*
honest	honnête	*oneht*
honey	le miel	*luh myehl*
horizontal	horizontal	*oareezawntahl*
horrible	horrible	*oareebl*
horse	le cheval	*luh shuhvahl*
hospital	l'hôpital (m.)	*loapeetahl*
hospitality	l'hospitalité (f.)	*lospeetahleetay*
hot	chaud	*shoa*
hot-water bottle	la bouillotte	*lah booy-yot*
hot (spicy)	pimenté	*peemohntay*
hotel	l'hôtel (m.)	*loatehl*
hour	l'heure (f.)	*luhr*
house	la maison	*lah mehzawn*
household appliances	les appareils	*lay zahpahrehy*
houses of parliament	le parlement	*luh pahrluhmohn*
housewife	la femme au foyer	*lah fahm oa fwahyay*
how far?	c'est loin?	*seh lwahn?*
how long?	combien de temps?	*kawnbyahn duh tohn?*
how much?	combien?	*kawnbyahn?*

how?	comment?	*komohn?*
hungry (to be)	avoir faim	*ahvwahr fahn*
hurricane	l'ouragan (m.)	*loorahgohn*
hurry	la hâte	*lah aht*
husband	le mari	*luh mahree*
hut	la cabane	*lah kahbahnn*
hyperventilation	l'hyperventilation (f.)	*leepehrvohnteelahsyawn*

I

ice cream	la glace	*lah glahs*
ice cubes	les glaçons	*lay glahsawn*
ice skate	patiner	*pahteenay*
idea	l'idée (f.)	*leeday*
identification	la pièce d'identité	*lah pyehs deedohnteetay*
identify	identifier	*eedohnteefyay*
ignition key	la clef de contact	*lah klay duh kawntahkt*
ill	malade	*mahlahd*
illness	la maladie	*lah mahlahdee*
imagine	imaginer	*eemahjheenay*
immediately	immédiatement	*eemaydyahtmohn*
import duty	les droits de douane	*lay drwah duh dwahnn*
impossible	impossible	*ahnposeebl*
in	dans	*dohn*
in the evening	le soir	*luh swahr*
in the morning	le matin	*luh mahtahn*
included	compris	*kawnpree*
indicate	indiquer	*ahndeekay*
indicator	le clignotant	*luh kleenyotohn*
inexpensive	bon marché	*bawn mahrshay*
infection (viral/ bacterial)	l'infection (virale/ bactérielle) (f.)	*lahnfehksyawn (veerahl, bahktayryehl)*
inflammation	l'inflammation (f.)	*lahnflahmahsyawn*
information	l'information (f.)	*lahnformahsyawn*
information	le renseignement	*luh rohnsehnymohn*
information office	le bureau de renseignements	*luh bewroa duh rohnsehnymohn*
injection	la piqûre	*lah peekewr*
injured	blessé	*blehssay*
inner ear	l'oreille interne (f.)	*lorehy ahntehrn*
inner tube	la chambre à air	*lah shohnbr ah ehr*
innocent	innocent	*eenosohn*
insect	l'insecte (m.)	*lahnsehkt*
insect bite	la piqûre d'insecte	*lah peekewr dahnsehkt*
insect repellant	l'huile contre les moustiques	*lweel kawntr lay moosteek*
inside	à l'intérieur	*ah lahntayryuhr*
instructions	le mode d'emploi	*luh mod dohnplwah*
insurance	l'assurance (f.)	*lahsewrohns*
intermission	la pause	*lah poaz*
international	international	*ahntehrnahsyonahl*
interpreter	l'interprète (m./f.)	*lahntehrpreht*
intersection	le carrefour	*luh kahrfoor*
introduce oneself	se présenter	*suh prayzohntay*
invite	inviter	*ahnveetay*

Word list

15

invoice	la facture	_lah fahktewr_
iodine	l'iode (m.)	_lyod_
Ireland	l'Irlande (f.)	_leerlohnd_
Irish	irlandais	_leerlohndeh_
iron (verb)	repasser	_ruhpahsay_
iron	le fer à repasser	_luh fehr ah ruhpahsay_
ironing board	la table à repasser	_lah tahbl ah ruhpahsay_
island	l'île (f.)	_leel_
it's a pleasure	je vous en prie	_jhuh voo zohn pree_
Italian	italien	_eetahlyahn_
itch	la démangeaison	_lah daymohnjhehzawn_

J

jack	le cric	_luh kreek_
jacket	la veste	_lah vehst_
jam	la confiture	_lah kawnfeetewr_
January	janvier	_jhohnvyay_
jaw	la mâchoire	_lah mahshwahr_
jellyfish	la méduse	_lah maydewz_
jeweller	le bijoutier	_luh beejhootyay_
jewellery	les bijoux	_lay beejhoo_
jog	faire du jogging	_fehr dew jogeeng_
joke	la blague	_lah blahg_
juice	le jus	_luh jhew_
July	juillet	_jhweeyeh_
jump leads	le câble de	_luh kahbl duh_
	démarrage	_daymahrahjh_
jumper	le pull-over	_luh pewlovehr_
June	juin	_jhwahn_

K

key	la clef/clé	_lah klay_
kilo	le kilo	_luh keeloa_
kilometre	le kilomètre	_luh keeloamehtr_
king	le roi	_luh rwah_
kiss (verb)	embrasser	_ohnbrahssay_
kiss	le baiser	_luh bayzay_
kitchen	la cuisine	_lah kweezeen_
knee	le genou	_luh jhuhnoo_
knee socks	les mi-bas	_lay mee bah_
knife	le couteau	_luh kootoa_
knit	tricoter	_treekotay_
know	savoir	_sahvwahr_

L

lace	la dentelle	_lah dohntehl_
ladies' toilets	les toilettes pour	_lay twahleht_
	dames	_poor dahm_
lake	le lac	_luh lahk_
lamp	la lampe	_lah lohnp_
land	atterrir	_ahtayreer_
lane	la voie	_lah vwah_
language	la langue	_lah lohng_
large	grand	_grohn_
last	dernier, passé	_dehrnyay, pahssay_
last night	la nuit passée	_lah nwee pahssay_

late	tard	*tahr*
later	tout à l'heure	*too tah luhr*
laugh	rire	*reer*
launderette	la laverie	*lah lahvree*
	automatique	*oatoamahteek*
law	la loi	*lah lwah*
laxative	le laxatif	*luh lahxahteef*
leaky	crevé	*kruhvay*
leather	le cuir	*luh kweer*
leather goods	les articles	*lay zahrteekl*
	de maroquinerie	*duh mahrokeenree*
leave	partir	*pahrteer*
leek	le poireau	*luh pwahroa*
left	gauche	*goash*
left luggage	la consigne	*lah kawnseeny*
left, on the	à gauche	*ah goash*
leg	la jambe	*lah jhohnb*
lemon	le citron	*luh seetrawn*
lemonade	la limonade	*lah leemonahd*
lend	prêter (à)	*prehtay (ah)*
lens	la lentille	*lah lohnteey*
lentils	les lentilles	*lay lohnteey*
less	moins	*mwahn*
lesson	la leçon	*lah luhsawn*
letter	la lettre	*lah lehtr*
lettuce	la laitue	*lah laytew*
level crossing	le passage à niveau	*luh pahssahjh ah*
		neevoa
library	la bibliothèque	*lah beebleeotehk*
lie (down)	s'étendre	*saytohndr*
lie (verb)	mentir	*mohnteer*
hitch-hiking	l'auto-stop	*loatoastop*
lift (in building)	l'ascenseur (m.)	*lahsohnsuhr*
lift (chair)	le télésiège	*luh taylaysyehjh*
light (not dark)	clair	*klehr*
light (not heavy)	léger	*layjhay*
light	la lumière	*lah lewmyehr*
lighter	le briquet	*luh breekeh*
lighthouse	le phare	*luh fahr*
lightning	la foudre	*lah foodr*
like	aimer	*aymay*
line	la ligne	*lah leenyuh*
linen	le lin	*luh lahn*
lipstick	le rouge à lèvres	*luh roojh ah lehvr*
liquorice	le réglisse	*luh rayglees*
listen	écouter	*aykootay*
literature	la littérature	*lah leetayrahtewr*
litre	le litre	*luh leetr*
little	peu	*puh*
live	habiter	*ahbeetay*
live	vivre	*veevr*
live together	habiter ensemble	*ahbeetay ohnsohnbl*
lobster	le homard	*luh omahr*
locally	localement	*lokahlmohn*
lock	la serrure	*lah sehrewr*
long	long	*lawn*
look	regarder	*ruhgahrday*

Word list

15

look for	chercher	*shehrshay*
look up	rechercher	*ruhshehrshay*
lorry	le camion	*luh kahmyawn*
lose	perdre	*pehrdr*
loss	la perte	*lah pehrt*
lost	introuvable, perdu	*ahntroovahbl, pehrdew*
lost item	l'objet perdu (m.)	*lohbjeh pehrdew*
lost property office	les objets trouvés	*lay zobjheh troovay*
lotion	la lotion	*lah loasyawn*
loud	fort	*for*
love (to be in)	être amoureux	*ehtr ahmooruh*
love (verb)	aimer	*aymay*
love	l'amour (m.)	*lahmoor*
low	bas	*bah*
low tide	le reflux	*luh ruhflew*
luck	la chance	*lah shohns*
luggage	le bagage	*luh bahgahjh*
luggage locker	la consigne automatique	*lah kawnseenyuh oatoamahteek*
lunch	le déjeuner	*luh dayjhuhnay*
lunchroom	le café	*luh kahfay*
lungs	les poumons	*lay poomawn*

M

macaroni	les macaronis	*lay mahkahroanee*
madam	madame	*mahdahm*
magazine	la revue	*lah ruhvew*
mail	le courrier	*luh kooryay*
main post office	le bureau de poste central	*luh bewroa duh post sohntral*
main road	la grande route	*lah grohnd root*
make an appointment	prendre un rendez-vous	*prohndr uhn rohndayvoo*
make love	faire l'amour	*fehr lahmoor*
makeshift	provisoirement	*proveezwahrmohn*
man	l'homme (m.)	*lom*
manager	le directeur	*luh deerehktuhr*
mandarin	la mandarine	*lah mohndahreen*
manicure	la manucure	*lah mahnewkewr*
map	la carte géographique	*lah kahrt jhayoagrahfeek*
marble	le marbre	*luh mahrbruh*
March	mars	*mahrs*
margarine	la margarine	*lah mahrgahreen*
marina	le port de plaisance	*luh por duh playzohns*
market	le marché	*luh mahrshay*
marriage	le mariage	*luh mahryajh*
married	marié	*mahreeay*
mass	la messe	*lah mehs*
massage	le massage	*luh mahsahjh*
mat	mat	*maht*
match	le match	*luh mahch*
matches	les allumettes	*lay zahlewmeht*
May	mai	*meh*
maybe	peut-être	*puh tehtr*
mayonnaise	la mayonnaise	*lah mahyonehz*
mayor	le maire	*luh mehr*

meal	le repas	*luh ruhpah*
mean	signifier	*seenyeefyay*
meat	la viande	*lah vyohnd*
medical insurance	l'assurance	*lahsewrohns*
	maladie (f.)	*mahlahdee*
medication	le médicament	*luh maydeekahmohn*
medicine	le médicament	*luh maydeekahmohn*
meet	rencontrer	*rohnkohntray*
melon	le melon	*luh muhlawn*
membership	l'adhésion (f.)	*lahdayzyawn*
menstruate	avoir ses règles	*ahvwahr say rehgl*
menstruation	les règles	*lay rehgl*
menu	la carte	*lah kahrt*
menu of the day	le menu du jour	*luh muhnew dew jhoor*
message	le message	*luh mehsahjh*
metal	le métal	*luh maytahl*
meter	le compteur	*luh kawntuhr*
metre	le mètre	*luh mehtr*
migraine	la migraine	*lah meegrehn*
mild (tobacco)	léger	*layjhay*
milk	le lait	*luh leh*
millimetre	le millimètre	*luh meeleemehtr*
milometer	le compteur	*luh kawntuhr*
	kilométrique	*keeloamaytreek*
mince	la viande hachée	*lah vyohnd ahshay*
mineral water	l'eau minérale (f.)	*loa meenayral*
minute	la minute	*lah meenewt*
mirror	le miroir	*luh meerwahr*
miss	manquer	*mohnkay*
missing (to be)	manquer	*mohnkay*
mistake	l'erreur (f.)	*lehruhr*
misunderstanding	le malentendu	*luh mahlohntohndew*
mocha	le moka	*luh mokah*
modern art	l'art moderne (m.)	*lahr modehrn*
molar	la molaire	*lah molehr*
moment	le moment	*luh momohn*
Monday	lundi	*luhndee*
money	l'argent (m.)	*lahrjhohn*
month	le mois	*luh mwah*
moped	le cyclomoteur	*luh seekloamotuhr*
morning-after pill	la pilule du	*lah peelewl dew*
	lendemain	*lohnduhmahn*
mosque	la mosquée	*lah moskay*
motel	le motel	*luh moatehl*
mother	la mère	*lah mehr*
moto-cross	le moto-cross	*luh moatoakros*
motorbike	la motocyclette	*lah moatoaseekleht*
motorboat	le bateau à moteur	*luh bahtoa ah motuhr*
motorway	l'autoroute (f.)	*loatoaroot*
mountain	la montagne	*lah mawntanyuh*
mountain hut	le refuge	*luh ruhfewjh*
mountaineering	l'alpinisme (m.)	*lahlpeeneesm*
mountaineering shoes	les chaussures	*lay shoasewr duh*
	de montagne	*mawntanyuh*
mouse	la souris	*lah sooree*
mouth	la bouche	*lah boosh*
much/many	beaucoup	*boakoo*

Word list

15

multi-storey car park	le parking	*luh pahrkeeng*
muscle	le muscle	*luh mewskl*
muscle spasms	les crampes	*lay krohnp*
	musculaires	*mewskewlehr*
museum	le musée	*luh mewzay*
mushrooms	les champignons	*lay shohnpeenyawn*
music	la musique	*lah mewzeek*
musical	la comédie musicale	*lah komaydee*
		mewzeekahl
mussels	les moules	*lay mool*
mustard	la moutarde	*lah mootahrd*

N

nail (on hand)	l'ongle (m.)	*lawngl*
nail	le clou	*luh kloo*
nail polish	le vernis à ongles	*luh vehrnee ah awngl*
nail polish remover	le dissolvant	*luh deesolvohn*
nail scissors	le coupe-ongles	*luh koop awngl*
naked	nu	*new*
nappy	la couche	*lah koosh*
nationality	la nationalité	*lah nahsyonahleetay*
natural	naturel	*nahtewrehl*
nature	la nature	*lah nahtewr*
naturism	le naturisme (m.)	*luh nahtewreesm*
nauseous	(avoir) mal au coeur	*(ahvwahr) mahl oa kuhr*
near	près	*preh*
nearby	tout près	*too preh*
necessary	nécessaire	*naysehsehr*
neck	le collier	*luh kolyay*
necklace	la chaîne	*lah shehn*
nectarine	la nectarine	*lah nehktahreen*
needle	l'aiguille (f.)	*laygweey*
negative	le négatif	*luh naygahteef*
neighbours	les voisins	*lay vwahzahn*
nephew	le neveu	*luh nuhvuh*
Netherlands	les Pays-Bas	*lay pehy bah*
never	jamais	*jhahmeh*
new	nouveau	*noovoa*
news	les informations	*lay zahnformahsyawn*
news stand	le kiosque	*luh kyosk*
newspaper	le journal	*luh jhoornahl*
next	le prochain	*luh proshahn*
next to	à côté de	*ah koatay duh*
nice (friendly)	gentil	*jhohntee*
nice	agréable, bon	*ahgrayahbl, bawn*
niece	la nièce	*lah nyehs*
night	la nuit	*lah nwee*
night duty	le service de nuit	*luh sehrvees duh nwee*
nightclub	la boîte de nuit/	*lah bwaht duh nwee/*
	le night-club	*luh naheet kluhb*
nightlife	la vie nocturne	*lah vee noktewrn*
nipple	la tétine	*lah tayteen*
no-one	personne	*pehrson*
no	non	*nawn*
no overtaking	l'interdiction	*lahntehrdeeksyawn*
	de dépasser (f.)	*duh daypahsay*
noise	le bruit	*luh brwee*

nonstop	continu	*kawnteenew*
normal	normal, ordinaire	*normahl, ordeenehr*
north	le nord	*luh nor*
nose	le nez	*luh nay*
nose bleed	le saignement de nez	*luh sehnyuhmohn dew nay*
nose drops	les gouttes pour le nez	*lay goot poor luh nay*
notepaper	le papier postal	*luh pahpyay postahl*
nothing	rien	*ryahn*
November	novembre	*novohnbr*
nowhere	nulle part	*newl pahr*
nudist beach	la plage de nudistes	*lah plahjh duh newdeest*
number	le numéro	*luh newmayroa*
number plate	la plaque d'immatriculation	*lah plahk deemahtree-kewlahsyawn*
nurse	l'infirmière (f.)	*lahnfeermyehr*
nutmeg	la noix de muscade	*lah nwah duh mewskahd*
nuts	les noix	*lay nwah*

O

October	octobre	*oktobr*
off licence	le marchand de vin	*luh mahrshohn duh vahn*
offer	offrir	*ofreer*
office	le bureau	*luh bewroa*
oil	l'huile (f.)	*lweel*
oil level	le niveau d'huile	*luh neevoa dweel*
ointment	le baume	*luh boam*
ointment for burns	la pommade contre les brûlures	*lah pomahd kawntr lay brewlewr*
okay	d'accord	*dahkor*
old	vieux	*vyuh*
old town	la vieille ville	*lah vyehy veel*
olive oil	l'huile d'olive	*lweel doleev*
olives	les olives	*lay zoleev*
omelette	l'omelette (f.)	*lomleht*
on	sur	*sewr*
on board	à bord	*ah bor*
on the way	en cours de route	*ohn koor duh root*
oncoming car	le véhicule en sens inverse	*luh vayeekewl ohn sohns ahnvehr*
one-way traffic	la circulation à sens unique	*lah seerkewlahsyawn ah sohns ewneek*
one hundred grams	cent grammes	*sohn grahm*
onion	l'oignon (m.)	*lonyawn*
open (verb)	ouvrir	*oovreer*
open	ouvert	*oovehr*
opera	l'opéra (m.)	*loapayrah*
operate	opérer	*oapayray*
operator (telephone)	la téléphoniste	*lah taylayfoneest*
operetta	l'opérette (f.)	*loapayreht*
opposite	en face	*ohn fahs*
optician	l'opticien (m.)	*lopteesyahn*
or	ou	*oo*

Word list

15

137

orange	l'orange (f.)	*lorohnjh*
orange (adj.)	orange	*orohnjh*
orange juice	le jus d'orange	*luh jhew dorohnjh*
order (verb)	commander	*komohnday*
order	la commande	*lah kohmohnd*
other	l'autre	*loatr*
other side	l'autre côté	*loatr koatay*
outside	dehors	*duh-or*
overtake	doubler	*dooblay*
oysters	les huîtres	*lay zweetr*

P

package (post)	le paquet postal	*luh pahkeh postahl*
packed lunch	le casse-croûte	*luh kahs kroot*
page	la page	*lah pahjh*
pain	la douleur	*lah dooluhr*
painkiller	le calmant	*luh kahlmohn*
paint	la peinture	*lah pahntewr*
painting (art)	le tableau	*luh tahbloa*
palace	le palais	*luh pahleh*
pan	la casserole	*lah kahsrol*
pancake	la crèpe	*lah krehp*
pane	la vitre	*lah veetr*
pants	la culotte	*lah kewlot*
panty liner	le protège-slip	*luh protehjh sleep*
paper	le papier	*luh pahpyay*
paraffin oil	le pétrole	*luh paytrol*
parasol	le parasol	*luh pahrahsol*
parcel	le colis	*luh kolee*
pardon	pardon	*pahrdawn*
parents	les parents	*lay pahrohn*
park	le parc	*luh pahrk*
park (verb)	garer	*gahray*
parking space	la place de parking	*lah plahs duh pahrkeeng*
parsley	le persil	*luh pehrsee*
part	la pièce	*lah pyehs*
partition	la séparation	*lah saypahrahsyawn*
partner	le/la partenaire	*luh/lah pahrtuhnehr*
party	la fête	*lah feht*
passable	praticable	*prahteekahbl*
passenger	le passager	*luh pahsahjhay*
passport	le passeport	*luh pahspor*
passport photo	la photo d'identité	*lah foatoa deedohnteetay*
patient	le patient	*luh pahsyohn*
pavement	le trottoir	*luh trotwahr*
pay	payer	*payay*
peach	la pêche	*lah pehsh*
peanuts	les cacahuètes	*lay kahkahweht*
pear	la poire	*lah pwahr*
peas	les petits pois	*lay puhtee pwah*
pedal	la pédale	*lah paydahl*
pedestrian crossing	le passage clouté	*luh pahsahjh klootay*
pedicure	le/la pédicure	*luh/lah paydeekewr*
pen	le stylo	*luh steeloa*
pencil	le crayon	*luh krayawn*

penis	le pénis	*luh paynees*
pepper (capsicum)	le poivron	*luh pwahvrawn*
pepper	le poivre	*luh pwahvr*
performance	la représentation de théâtre	*lah ruhprayzohntahsyawn duh tayahtr*
perfume	le parfum	*luh pahrfuhn*
perm (verb)	faire une permanente à	*fehr ewn pehrmahnohnt ah*
perm	la permanente	*lah pehrmahnohnt*
permit	le permis	*luh pehrmee*
person	la personne	*lah pehrson*
personal	personnel	*pehrsonehl*
petrol	l'essence (f.)	*lehssohns*
petrol station	la station-service	*lah stahsyawn sehrvees*
pets	les animaux domestiques	*lay zahneemoa domehsteek*
pharmacy	la pharmacie	*lah fahrmahsee*
phone (by)	par téléphone	*pahr taylayfon*
phone (tele-)	le téléphone	*luh taylayfon*
phone (verb)	téléphoner	*taylayfonay*
phone box	la cabine téléphonique	*lah kahbeen taylayfoneek*
phone directory	l'annuaire	*lahnnewehr*
phone number	le numéro de téléphone	*luh newmayroa duh taylayfon*
photo	la photo	*la foatoa*
photocopier	le photocopieur	*luh foatoakopyuhr*
photocopy (verb)	photocopier	*foatoakopyay*
photocopy	la photocopie	*lah foatoakopee*
pick up	aller chercher	*ahlay shehrshay*
picnic	le pique-nique	*luh peek neek*
pier	la jetée	*lah jhuhtay*
pigeon	le pigeon	*luh peejhyawn*
pill (contraceptive)	la pilule	*lah peelewl*
pillow	le coussin	*luh koossahn*
pillowcase	la taie d'oreiller	*lah tay dorehyay*
pin	l'épingle (f.)	*laypahngl*
pineapple	l'ananas (m.)	*lahnahnahs*
pipe	la pipe	*lah peep*
pipe tobacco	le tabac à pipe	*luh tahbah ah peep*
pity	dommage	*domahjh*
places of entertainment	les possibilités de sortie	*lay poseebeeleetay duh sortee*
places of interest	les curiosités	*lay kewryozeetay*
plan	l'intention (f.)	*lahntohnsyawn*
plant	la plante	*lah plohnt*
plaster	le sparadrap	*luh spahrahdrah*
plastic	plastique	*plahsteek*
plastic bag	le sac en plastique	*luh sahk ohn plahsteek*
plate	l'assiette (f.)	*lahsyeht*
platform	la voie, le quai	*lah vwah, luh kay*
play (theatre)	la pièce de théâtre	*lah pyehs duh tayahtr*
play (verb)	jouer	*jhooay*
play basketball	jouer au basket	*jhooay oa bahskeht*
play billiards	jouer au billiard	*jhooay oa biy-yahr*

Word list

15

play chess	jouer aux échecs	*jhooay oa zayshehk*
play draughts	jouer aux dames	*jhooay oa dahm*
play golf	jouer au golf	*jhooay oa golf*
playing cards	les cartes à jouer	*lay kahrt ah jhooay*
pleasant	agréable	*ahgrayahbl*
please	s'il vous plaît	*seel voo pleh*
pleasure	la satisfaction	*lah sahteesfahksyawn*
plum	la prune	*lah prewn*
pocketknife	le canif	*luh kahneef*
point	indiquer	*ahndeekay*
poison	le poison	*luh pwahzawn*
police	la police	*lah polees*
police station	le poste de police	*luh post duh polees*
policeman	l'agent de police (m.)	*lahjhohn duh polees*
pond	le bassin	*luh bahsahn*
pony	le poney	*luh poaneh*
pop concert	le concert pop	*luh kawnsehr pop*
population	la population	*lah popewlahsyawn*
pork	la viande de porc	*lah vyohnd duh por*
port	le porto	*luh portoa*
porter	le porteur	*luh portuhr*
post code	le code postal	*luh kod postahl*
post office	la poste	*lah post*
postage	le port	*luh por*
postbox	la boîte aux lettres	*lah bwaht oa lehtr*
postcard	la carte postale	*lah kahrt postahl*
postman	le facteur	*luh fahktuhr*
potato	la pomme de terre	*lah pom duh tehr*
poultry	la volaille	*lah vohlahy*
pound	la livre	*lah leevr*
powdered milk	le lait en poudre	*luh leh ohn poodr*
prawns	les crevettes roses	*lay kruhveht roaz*
precious	précieux	*praysyuh*
prefer	préférer	*prayfayray*
preference	la préférence	*lah prayfayrohns*
pregnant	enceinte	*ohnsahnt*
present (adj.)	présent	*prayzohn*
present	le cadeau	*luh kahdoa*
press	appuyer	*ahpweeyay*
pressure	la pression	*lah prehsyawn*
price	le prix	*luh pree*
price list	la liste de prix	*lah leest duh pree*
print (verb)	faire tirer	*fehr teeray*
print	l'épreuve (f.)	*laypruhv*
probably	probablement	*probahbluhmohn*
problem	le problème	*luh problehm*
profession	la profession	*lah profehsyawn*
programme	le programme	*luh prograhm*
pronounce	prononcer	*proanawnsay*
propane gas	le gaz propane	*luh gahz propahn*
pull	arracher	*ahrahshay*
pull a muscle	froisser un muscle	*frwahsay uhn mewskl*
pure	pur	*pewr*
purple	violet	*veeoleh*
purse	le porte-monnaie	*luh port moneh*
push	pousser	*poossay*
pushchair	la poussette	*lah poosseht*

| puzzle | le puzzle | *luh puhzl* |
| pyjamas | le pyjama | *luh peejhahmah* |

Q

quarter	le quart	*luh kahr*
quarter of an hour	le quart d'heure	*luh kahr duhr*
queen	la reine	*lah rehn*
question	la question	*lah kehstyawn*
quick	rapide	*rahpeed*
quiet	tranquille	*trohnkeey*

R

radio	la radio	*lah rahdyoa*
railways	les chemins de fer (m.)	*lay shuhmahn duh fehr*
rain (verb)	pleuvoir	*pluhvwahr*
rain	la pluie	*lah plwee*
raincoat	l'imperméable (m.)	*lahnpehrmayahbl*
raisins	les raisins secs	*lay rehzahn sehk*
rape	le viol	*luh vyol*
rapids	le courant rapide	*luh koorohn rahpeed*
raspberries	les framboises	*lay frohnbwahz*
raw	cru	*krew*
raw ham	le jambon cru	*luh jhohnbawn krew*
raw vegetables	les crudités	*lay krewdeetay*
razor blades	les lames de rasoir	*lay lahm duh rahzwahr*
read (verb)	lire	*leer*
ready	prêt	*preh*
really	vraiment	*vrehmohn*
receipt (till)	le ticket de caisse	*luh teekeh duh kehs*
receipt	le reçu, la quittance	*luh ruhsew, lah keetohns*
recipe	la recette	*lah ruhseht*
reclining chair	la chaise longue	*lah shehz lawng*
recommend	recommander	*ruhkomohnday*
recovery service	l'assistance routiere (f.)	*lahseestohns rootyehr*
rectangle	le rectangle	*luh rehktohngl*
red	rouge	*roojh*
red wine	le vin rouge	*luh vahn roojh*
reduction	la réduction	*lah raydewksyawn*
refrigerator	le réfrigérateur	*luh rayfreejhayrahtuhr*
regards	les amitiés	*lay zahmeetyay*
region	la région	*lah rayjhyawn*
registration	la carte grise	*lah kahrt greez*
relatives	la famille	*lah fahmeey*
reliable	sûr	*sewr*
religion	la religion	*lah ruhleejhyawn*
rent out	louer	*looay*
repair (verb)	réparer	*raypahray*
repairs	la réparation	*lah raypahrahsyawn*
repeat	répéter	*raypaytay*
report	le procès-verbal	*luh proseh vehrbahl*
resent	prendre mal	*prohndr mahl*
responsible	responsable	*rehspawnsahbl*
rest	se reposer	*suh ruhpoazay*
restaurant	le restaurant	*luh rehstoarohn*

Word list **15**

result	le résultat	*luh rayzewltah*
retired	à la retraite	*ah lah ruhtreht*
retirement	la retraite	*lah ruhtreht*
return (ticket)	l'aller-retour (m.)	*lahlay ruhtoor*
reverse (vehicle)	faire marche arrière	*fehr mahrsh ahryehr*
rheumatism	le rhumatisme	*luh rewmahteesm*
rice	le riz	*luh ree*
ridiculous	ridicule	*reedeekewl*
riding (horseback)	faire du cheval	*fehr dew shuhvahl*
riding school	le manège	*luh mahnehjh*
right	la droite	*lah drwaht*
right of way	la priorité	*lah preeoreetay*
right, on the	à droite	*ah drwaht*
ripe	mûr	*mewr*
risk	le risque	*luh reesk*
river	la rivière	*reevyehr*
road	la route	*lah root*
roasted	rôti	*roatee*
rock	le rocher	*luh roshay*
roll	le petit pain	*luh puhtee pahn*
rolling tobacco	le tabac à rouler	*luh tahbah ah roolay*
roof rack	la galerie	*lah gahlree*
room	la pièce	*lah pyehs*
room number	le numéro de chambre	*luh newmayroa duh shohnbr*
room service	le service de chambre	*luh sehrvees duh shohnbr*
rope	la corde	*lah kord*
rose	la rose	*lah roaz*
rosé	le rosé	*luh roazay*
roundabout	le rond-point	*luh rawn pwahn*
route	l'itinéraire (m.)	*leeteenayrehr*
rowing boat	la barque	*la bahrk*
rubber	le caoutchouc	*luh kah-oochoo*
rubbish	les détritus	*luh daytreetews*
rucksack	le sac à dos	*luh sahk ah doa*
rude	mal élevé	*mahl aylvay*
ruins	les ruines (f.)	*lay rween*
run into	rencontrer	*rohnkawntray*
running shoes	les chaussures de sport	*lay shoasewr duh spor*

s

sad	triste	*treest*
safari	le safari	*luh sahfahree*
safe (adj.)	en sécurité	*ohn saykewreetay*
safe	le coffre-fort	*luh kofr for*
safety pin	l'épingle de nourrice (f.)	*laypahngl duh noorees*
sail	faire de la voile	*fehr duh lah vwahl*
sailing boat	le voilier	*luh vwahlyay*
salad	la salade	*lah sahlahd*
salad oil	l'huile de table (f.)	*lweel duh tahbl*
salami	le salami	*luh sahlahmee*
sale	les soldes	*lay sold*
salt	le sel	*luh sehl*
same	le même	*luh mehm*

Word list

15

sandwich	le sandwich	*luh sohndweech*
sandy beach	la plage de sable	*lah plahjh duh sahbl*
sanitary towel	la serviette	*lah sehrvyeht*
	hygiénique	*eejhyayneek*
sardines	les sardines	*lay sahrdeen*
satisfied	content (de)	*kawntohn (duh)*
Saturday	samedi	*sahmdee*
sauce	la sauce	*lah soas*
sauna	le sauna	*luh soanah*
sausage	la saucisse	*lah soasees*
savoury	salé	*sahlay*
say	dire	*deer*
scarf	l'écharpe (f.)	*layshahrp*
scenic walk	le circuit pédestre	*luh seerkwee*
		paydehstr
school	l'école (f.)	*laykol*
scissors	les ciseaux	*lay seezoa*
scooter	le scooter	*luh skootehr*
scorpion	le scorpion	*luh skorpyawn*
Scotland	l'Ecosse (f.)	*laykos*
Scottish	écossais	*aykosseh*
scrambled eggs	l'oeuf brouillé (m.)	*lef brooy-yay*
screw	la vis	*lah vees*
screwdriver	le tournevis	*luh toornuhvees*
sculpture	la sculpture	*lah skewltewr*
sea	la mer	*lah mehr*
seasick (to be)	avoir le mal de	*ahvwahr luh mahl duh*
	mer	*mehr*
seat	la place	*lah plahs*
second-hand	d'occasion	*dokahzyawn*
second (adj.)	deuxième	*duhzyehm*
second	la seconde	*lah suhgawnd*
sedative	le tranquillisant	*luh trohnkeeleezohn*
self-timer	le déclencheur	*luh dayklohnshuhr*
	automatique	*oatoamahteek*
semi-skimmed	demi-écrémé	*duhmee aykraymay*
send	expédier	*ehxpaydyay*
sentence	la phrase	*lah frahz*
separated	séparé	*saypahray*
September	septembre	*sehptohnbr*
serious	sérieux	*sayryuh*
service	le service	*luh sehrvees*
serviette	la serviette	*lah sehrvyeht*
set (hair)	faire une mise en plis	*fehr ewn meez ohn*
		plee
sewing thread	le fil à coudre	*luh feel ah koodr*
shade	l'ombre (f.)	*lawnbr*
shallow	peu profond	*puh profawn*
shampoo	le shampooing	*luh shohnpwahn*
shark	le requin	*luh ruhkahn*
shave (verb)	se raser	*suh rahzay*
shaver	le rasoir électrique	*luh rahzwahr*
		aylehktreek
shaving brush	le blaireau	*luh blayroa*
shaving cream	la crème à raser	*lah krehm ah rahzay*
shaving soap	le savon à raser	*luh sahvawn ah rahzay*
sheet	le drap	*luh drah*

Word list

15

143

sherry	le xérès	*luh ksayrehz*
shirt	la chemise	*lah shuhmeez*
shoe	la chaussure	*lah shoasewr*
shoe polish	le cirage	*luh seerajh*
shoe shop	le magasin de chaussures	*luh mahgahzahn duh shoasewr*
shoelace	le lacet	*luh lahseh*
shoemaker	le cordonnier	*luh kordonyay*
shop (verb)	faire les courses	*fehr lay koors*
shop	le magasin	*luh mahgahzahn*
shop assistant	la vendeuse	*lah vohnduhz*
shop window	la vitrine	*lah veetreen*
shopping bag	le cabas	*luh kahbah*
shopping centre	le centre commercial	*luh sohntr komehrsyahl*
short	court	*koor*
short circuit	le court-circuit	*luh koor seerkwee*
shorts	le bermuda	*luh behrmewdah*
shoulder	l'épaule (f.)	*laypoal*
show	le spectacle	*luh spehktahkl*
shower	la douche	*lah doosh*
shutter	l'obturateur (m.)	*lobtewrahtuhr*
sieve	la passoire	*lah pahswahr*
sign (verb)	signer	*seenyay*
sign	le panneau	*luh pahnoa*
signature	la signature	*lah seenyahtewr*
silence	le silence	*luh seelohns*
silver	l'argent (m.)	*lahrjhohn*
silver-plated	argenté	*ahrjhohntay*
simple	simple	*sahnpl*
single (ticket)	l'aller simple (m.)	*lahlay sahnpl*
single (unmarried)	célibataire	*sayleebahtehr*
single	le célibataire	*luh sayleebahtehr*
sir	monsieur	*muhsyuh*
sister	la soeur	*lah suhr*
sit (verb)	s'asseoir	*sahswahr*
size	la pointure, la taille	*lah pwahntewr, lah tahy*
ski (verb)	skier, faire du ski	*skeeay, fehr dew skee*
ski boots	les chaussures de ski	*lay shoasewr duh skee*
ski goggles	les lunettes de ski	*lay lewneht duh skee*
ski instructor	le moniteur de ski	*luh moneetuhr duh skee*
ski lessons/class	le cours de ski, la classe de ski	*luh koor duh skee, lah klahs duh skee*
ski lift	le remonte-pente	*luh ruhmawnt pohnt*
ski pants	le pantalon de ski	*luh pohntahlawn duh skee*
ski pass	le forfait de ski	*luh forfeh duh skee*
ski slope	la piste de ski	*lah peest duh skee*
ski stick	le bâton de ski	*luh bahtawn duh skee*
ski suit	la combinaison de ski	*lah kawnbeenehzawn duh skee*
ski wax	le fart à ski	*luh fahr ah skee*
skimmed	écrémé	*aykraymay*
skin	la peau	*lah poa*
skirt	la jupe	*lah jhewp*
skis	les skis	*lay skee*

sledge	la luge	*lah lewjh*
sleep (verb)	dormir	*dormeer*
sleep well	dormez-bien	*dormay byahn*
sleeping car	le wagon-lit	*luh vahgawn lee*
sleeping pills	les somnifères	*lay somneefehr*
slide	la diapositive	*lah deeahpozeeteev*
slim	mince	*mahns*
slip	la combinaison	*lah kawnbeenehzawn*
slip road	la bretelle d'accès	*lah bruhtehl dahkseh*
slow	lentement	*lohntuhmohn*
small	petit	*puhtee*
small change	la monnaie	*lah moneh*
smell (verb)	puer	*peway*
smoke	la fumée	*lah fewmay*
smoke (verb)	fumer	*fewmay*
smoked	fumé	*fewmay*
smoking compartment	le compartiment fumeurs	*luh kawnpahrteemohn fewmuhr*
snake	le serpent	*luh sehrpohn*
snorkel	le tuba	*luh tewbah*
snow (verb)	neiger	*nehjhay*
snow	la neige	*lah nehjh*
snow chains	les chaînes	*lay shehn*
soap	le savon	*luh sahvawn*
soap box	la boîte à savon	*lah bwaht ah sahvawn*
soccer (play)	jouer au football, le football	*jhooay oa footbol, luh footbol*
soccer match	le match de football	*luh mahch duh footbol*
socket	la prise	*lah preez*
socks	les chaussettes	*lay shoasseht*
soft drink	la boisson fraîche	*lah bwahssawn frehsh*
sole (fish)	la sole	*lah sol*
sole (shoe)	la semelle	*lah suhmehl*
solicitor	l'avocat	*lahvoakah*
someone	quelqu'un	*kehlkuhn*
something	quelque chose	*kehlkuhshoaz*
sometimes	parfois	*pahrfwah*
somewhere	quelque part	*kehlkuhpahr*
son	le fils	*luh fees*
soon	bientôt	*byahntoa*
sorbet	le sorbet	*luh sorbeh*
sore (be)	faire mal	*fehr mal*
sore throat	le mal de gorge	*luh mahl duh gorjh*
sorry	pardon	*pahrdawn*
sort	la sorte	*lah sort*
soup	la soupe	*lah soop*
sour	acide	*ahseed*
sour cream	la crème fraîche	*lah krehm frehsh*
source	la source	*lah soors*
south	le sud	*luh sewd*
souvenir	le souvenir	*luh soovneer*
spaghetti	les spaghetti	*lay spahgehtee*
spanner (open-ended)	las clé plate	*lay klay plaht*
spanner	la clef à molette	*lah klay ah moleht*
spare parts	les pièces détachées	*lay pyehs daytashay*

spare tyre	le pneu de rechange	*luh pnuh duh ruhshohnjh*
spare wheel	la roue de secours	*lah roo duh suhkoor*
speak (verb)	parler	*pahrlay*
special	spécial	*spaysyahl*
specialist	le spécialiste	*luh spaysyahleest*
specialty	la spécialité	*lah spaysyahleetay*
speed limit	la vitesse maximum	*lah veetehs mahxeemuhm*
spell (verb)	épeler	*aypuhlay*
spices	les épices	*lay zaypees*
spicy	épicé	*aypeesay*
splinter	l'écharde (f.)	*layshahrd*
spoon	la cuillère	*lah kweeyehr*
spoonful	la cuillerée	*lah kweeyuhray*
sport	le sport	*luh spor*
sports centre	la salle de sport	*lah sahl duh spohr*
spot	l'endroit (m.)	*lohndrwah*
sprain	fouler	*foolay*
spring	le printemps	*luh prahntohn*
square	le carré	*luh kahray*
square (town)	la place	*lah plahs*
square metre	le mètre carré	*luh mehtr kahray*
squash	le squash	*luh skwahsh*
stadium	le stade	*luh stahd*
stain	la tache	*lah tahsh*
stain remover	le détachant	*luh daytahshohn*
stairs	l'escalier (m.)	*lehskahlyay*
stalls	la salle	*lah sahl*
stamp	le timbre	*luh tahnbr*
start (verb)	démarrer	*daymahray*
station	la gare	*lah gahr*
statue	la statue	*lah stahtew*
stay (lodge)	loger	*lohjhay*
stay (remain)	rester	*rehstay*
stay	le séjour	*luh sayjhoor*
steal	voler	*volay*
steel	acier	*ahsyay*
stench	la mauvaise odeur	*lah moavehz oduhr*
sting	piquer	*peekay*
stitch (med.)	la suture	*lah sewtewr*
stitch (verb)	suturer	*sewtewray*
stock	le consommé	*luh kawnsomay*
stockings	les bas	*lay bah*
stomach	l'estomac (m.)	*lehstomah*
stomach	le ventre	*luh vohntr*
stomach ache	mal au ventre	*mahl oa vohntr*
stomach ache	le mal d'estomac	*luh mahl dehstomah*
stomach cramps	les spasmes abdominaux	*lay spahzm zahbdomeenoa*
stools	les selles	*lay sehl*
stop	arrêter	*ahrehtay*
stop	l'arrêt (m.)	*lahreh*
stopover	l'escale (f.)	*lehskahl*
storm	la tempête	*lah tohnpeht*
straight	raide	*rehd*
straight ahead	tout droit	*too drwah*

straw	la paille	*lah pahy*
street	la rue	*lah rew*
street (side)	côté rue	*koatay rew*
strike	la grève	*lah grehv*
study	faire des études	*fehr day zaytewd*
subscriber's number	le numéro d'abonné	*luh newmayroa dahbonay*
subtitled	sous-titré	*soo teetray*
succeed	réussir	*rayewsseer*
sugar	le sucre	*luh sewkr*
sugar lumps	les morceaux de sucre	*lay morsoa duh sewkr*
suit	le costume	*luh kostewm*
suitcase	la valise	*lah vahleez*
summer	l'été (m.)	*laytay*
summertime	l'heure d'été (f.)	*luhr daytay*
sun	le soleil	*luh solehy*
sun hat	le chapeau de soleil	*luh shahpoa duh solehy*
sun hat	le bonnet	*luh boneh*
sunbathe	prendre un bain de soleil	*prohndr uhn bahn duh solehy*
sunburn	le coup de soleil	*luh koo duh solehy*
Sunday	dimanche	*deemohnsh*
sunglasses	les lunettes de soleil	*lay lewneht duh solehy*
sunrise	le lever du soleil	*luh luhvay duh solehy*
sunset	le coucher du soleil	*luh kooshay duh solehy*
suntan lotion	la crème solaire	*lah krehm solehr*
suntan oil	l'huile solaire (f.)	*lweel sohlehr*
supermarket	le supermarché	*luh sewpehrmahrshay*
surcharge	le supplément	*luh sewplaymohn*
surf board	la planche à voile	*lah plohnsh ah vwahl*
surgery	la consultation	*lah kawnsewltahsyawn*
surname	le nom	*luh nawn*
surprise	la surprise	*lah sewrpreez*
swallow	avaler	*ahvahlay*
swamp	le marais	*luh mahreh*
sweat	la transpiration	*lah trohnspeerahsyawn*
sweet	le bonbon	*luh bawnbawn*
sweet (kind)	gentil	*jhohntee*
sweet (adj.)	sucré	*sewkray*
sweetcorn	le maïs	*luh mahees*
sweets	les friandises	*lay freeohndeez*
swim	nager	*nahjhay*
swimming pool	la piscine	*lah peeseen*
swimming trunks	le maillot de bain	*luh mahyoa duh bahn*
swindle	l'escroquerie (f.)	*lehskrokree*
switch	l'interrupteur (m.)	*lahntayrewptuhr*
synagogue	la synagogue	*lah seenahgog*

T

table	la table	*lah tahbl*
table tennis	jouer au ping-pong	*jhooay oa peeng pawng*
tablet	le comprimé	*luh kawnpreemay*
take (use)	utiliser	*ewteeleezay*
take	prendre	*prohndr*
take (time)	durer	*dewray*
take pictures	photographier	*foatoagrahfyay*

Word list

147

taken	occupé	*okewpay*
talcum powder	le talc	*luh tahlk*
talk	parler	*pahrlay*
tall	grand	*grohn*
tampons	les tampons	*lay tohnpawn*
tanned	brun	*bruhn*
tap	le robinet	*luh robeeneh*
tap water	l'eau du robinet (f.)	*loa dow roboonoh*
tartlet	la tartelette	*lah tahrtuhleht*
taste	goûter	*gootay*
tax free shop	le magasin	*luh mahgahzahn*
	hors-taxes	*or tahx*
taxi	le taxi	*luh tahxee*
taxi stand	la station de taxis	*lah stahsyawn duh tahxee*
tea	le thé	*luh tay*
teapot	la théière	*lah tay-yehr*
teaspoon	la petite cuillère	*lah puhteet kweeyehr*
telegram	le télégramme	*luh taylaygrahm*
telephoto lens	le téléobjectif	*luh taylayobjhehkteef*
television	la télévision	*lah taylayveezyawn*
telex	le télex	*luh taylehx*
temperature	la température	*lah tohnpayrahtewr*
temporary filling	le plombage	*luh plawnbahjh*
	provisoire	*proveezwahr*
tender	tendre	*tohndr*
tennis (play)	jouer au tennis	*jhooay oa taynees*
tennis ball	la balle de tennis	*lah bahl duh taynees*
tennis court	le court de tennis	*luh koor duh taynees*
tennis racket	la raquette de tennis	*lah rahkeht duh taynees*
tent	la tente	*lah tohnt*
tent peg	le piquet	*luh peekay*
terrace	la terrasse	*lah tehrahs*
terrible	épouvantable	*aypoovohntahbl*
thank	remercier	*ruhmehrsyay*
thank you	merci bien	*mehrsee byahn*
thanks	merci	*mehrsee*
thaw	dégeler	*dayjhuhlay*
theatre	le théâtre	*luh tayahtr*
theft	le vol	*luh vol*
there	là	*lah*
thermal bath	le bain thermal	*luh bahn tehrmahl*
thermometer	le thermomètre	*luh tehrmomehtr*
thick	gros	*groa*
thief	le voleur	*luh voluhr*
thigh	la cuisse	*lah kwees*
thin	maigre	*mehgr*
think	penser	*pohnsay*
third	le tiers	*luh tyehr*
thirsty, to be	la soif	*lah swahf*
this afternoon	cet après-midi	*seht ahpreh meedee*
this evening	ce soir	*suh swahr*
this morning	ce matin	*suh mahtahn*
thread	le fil	*luh feel*
throat	la gorge	*lah gorjh*

throat lozenges	les pastilles	*lay pahsteey*
	pour la gorge	*poor lah gorjh*
throw up	vomir	*vomeer*
thunderstorm	l'orage (m.)	*lorajh*
Thursday	jeudi	*jhuhdee*
ticket (admission)	le billet	*luh beeyeh*
ticket (travel)	le ticket	*luh teekeh*
tickets	les billets	*lay beeyeh*
tidy	ranger	*rohnjhay*
tie	la cravate	*lah krahvaht*
tights	le collant	*luh kolohn*
time (clock)	l'heure (f.)	*luhr*
time (occasion)	la fois	*lah fwah*
timetable	l'horaire des arrivées	*lorehr day zahreevay*
	et des départs	*ay day daypahr*
tin	la boîte de conserve	*lah bwaht duh*
		kawnsehrv
tip	le pourboire	*luh poorbwahr*
tissues	les mouchoirs	*lay mooshwahr*
	en papier	*ohn pahpyay*
toast	le toast	*luh toast*
tobacco	le tabac	*luh tahbah*
toboggan	la luge	*lah lewjh*
today	aujourd'hui	*oajhoordwee*
toe	l'orteil (m.)	*lortehy*
together	ensemble	*ohnsohnbl*
toilet	les toilettes	*lay twahleht*
toilet paper	le papier hygiénique	*luh pahpyay*
		eejhyayneek
toiletries	les articles de	*lay zahrteekl duh*
	toilette	*twahleht*
tomato	la tomate	*lah tomaht*
tomato purée	le concentré	*luh kawnsohntray*
	de tomates	*duh tomaht*
tomato sauce	le ketchup	*luh kehtchuhp*
tomorrow	demain	*duhmahn*
tongue	la langue	*lah lohng*
tonic water	le tonic	*luh toneek*
tonight	ce soir	*suh swahr*
tonight	cette nuit	*seht nwee*
too much	trop	*troa*
tools	les outils	*lay zootee*
tooth	la dent	*lah dohn*
toothache	le mal de dents	*luh mahl duh dohn*
toothbrush	la brosse à dents	*lah bros ah dohn*
toothpaste	le dentifrice	*luh dohnteefrees*
toothpick	le cure-dent	*luh kewrdohn*
top up	remplir	*rohnpleer*
total	le total	*luh totahl*
tough	dur	*dewr*
tour	le tour	*luh toor*
tour guide	le guide	*luh geed*
tourist card	la carte touristique	*lah kahrt tooreesteek*
tourist class	la classe touriste	*lah klahs tooreest*
Tourist Information office	l'office de tourisme	*lofees duh tooreesm*
tow	remorquer	*ruhmorkay*

tow cable	le câble	luh kahbl
towel	la serviette de toilette	lah sehrvyeht duh twahleht
tower	la tour	lah toor
town	la ville	lah veel
town hall	la mairie	lah mayree
toy	le jouet	luh jhooeh
traffic	la circulation	lah seerkewlahsyawn
traffic light	le feu de signalisation	luh fuh duh seenyahleezahsyawn
train	le train	luh trahn
train ticket	le billet de train	luh beeyeh duh trahn
train timetable	l'indicateur des chemins de fer	lahndeekahtuhr day shuhmahn duh fehr
translate	traduire	trahdweer
travel	voyager	vwahyahjhay
travel agent	l'agence de voyages (f.)	lahjhohns duh vwahyahjh
travel guide	le guide touristique	luh geed tooreesteek
traveller	le voyageur	luh vwahyahjhuhr
traveller's cheque	le chèque de voyage	luh shehk duh vwahyahjh
treacle	la mélasse	lah maylahs
treatment	le traitement	luh trehtmohn
triangle	le triangle	luh treeohngl
trim	tailler	tahy-yay
trip	l'excursion (f.)	lehxkewrsyawn
trip	le voyage	luh vwahyahjh
trout	la truite	lah trweet
trunk call	interurbain	ahntehrewrbahn
trunk code	l'indicatif (m.)	lahndeekahteef
trustworthy	de confiance	duh kawnfyohns
try on	essayer	ehsay-yay
tube	le tube	luh tewb
Tuesday	mardi	mahrdee
tumble drier	le sèche-linge	luh sahsh lahnjh
tuna	le thon	luh tawn
tunnel	le tunnel	luh tewnehl
TV	la télé	lah taylay
tweezers	la pince	lah pahns
tyre	le pneu	luh pnuh
tyre lever	le démonte-pneu	luh daymawnt pnuh
tyre pressure	la pression des pneus	lah prehsyawn day pnuh

U

ugly	laid	leh
umbrella	le parapluie	luh pahrahplwee
under	sous	soo
underground	le métro	luh maytroa
underground railway system	le réseau métropolitain	luh rayzoa maytroapoleetahn
underground station	la station de métro	lah stahsyawn duh maytroa
underpants	le slip	luh sleep
understand	comprendre	kawnprohndr
underwear	les sous-vêtements	lay soovehtmohn

Word list

15

undress	(se) déshabiller	*suh dayzahbeeyay*
unemployed	au chômage	*oa shoamahjh*
uneven	irrégulier	*eeraygewlyay*
university	l'université (f.)	*lewneevehrseetay*
unleaded	sans plomb	*sohn plawn*
up	en haut	*ohn oa*
urgent	urgent	*ewrjhohn*
urine	l'urine (f.)	*lewreen*
usually	généralement	*jhaynayrahlmohn*

V

vacate	évacuer	*ayvahkeway*
vaccinate	vacciner	*vahkseenay*
vagina	le vagin	*luh vahjhahn*
vaginal infection	l'infection	*lahnfehksyawn*
	vaginale	*vahjheenahl*
valid	valable	*vahlahbl*
valley	la vallée	*lah vahlay*
van	la camionnette	*lah kahmyoneht*
vanilla	la vanille	*lah vahneey*
vase	le vase	*luh vahz*
vaseline	la vaseline	*lah vahzleen*
veal	la viande de veau	*lah vyohnd duh voa*
vegetable soup	la soupe de légumes	*lah soop duh laygewm*
vegetables	le légume	*luh laygewm*
vegetarian	le végétarien	*luh vayjhaytahryahn*
vein	la veine	*lah vehn*
vending machine	le distributeur	*luh deestreebewtuhr*
venereal disease	la maladie	*lah mahlahdee*
	vénérienne	*vaynayryehn*
via	par	*pahr*
video recorder	le magnétoscope	*luh manyehtoskop*
video tape	la bande vidéo	*lah bohnd veedayoa*
view	la vue	*lah vew*
village	le village	*luh veelahjh*
visa	le visa	*luh veezah*
visit (verb)	rendre visite à	*rohndr veezeet ah*
visit	la visite	*lah veezeet*
vitamin tablet	le comprimé de	*luh kawnpreemay*
	vitamines	*duh veetahmeen*
vitamin	la vitamine	*lah veetahmeen*
volcano	le volcan	*luh volkohn*
volleyball	jouer au volley	*jhooay oa volay*
vomit	vomir	*vomeer*

W

wait	attendre	*ahtohndr*
waiter	le serveur	*luh sehrvuhr*
waiting room	la salle d'attente	*lah sahl dahtohnt*
waitress	la serveuse	*lah sehrvuhz*
wake up	réveiller	*rayvay-yay*
walk	la promenade	*lah promnahd*
walk (verb)	se promener	*suh promnay*
	marcher	*mahrshay*
wallet	le portefeuille	*luh portuhfuhy*
wardrobe	la garde-robe	*lah gahrd rob*
warm	chaud	*shoa*

warn	prévenir	*prayvuhneer*
warning	l'avertissement (m.)	*lahvehrteesmohn*
wash	laver	*lahvay*
washing-powder	le détergent	*luh daytehrjhohn*
washing	le linge	*luh lahnjh*
washing line	la corde à linge	*lah kord ah lahnjh*
washing machine	la machine à laver	*lah mahsheen ah lahvay*
wasp	la guêpe	*lah gehp*
water	l'eau (f.)	*loa*
water ski	faire du ski nautique	*fehr dew skee noateek*
waterproof	imperméable	*ahnpehrmayahbl*
wave-pool	la piscine à vagues artificielles	*lah peeseen ah vahg zahrteefeesyehl*
way	le moyen	*luh mwahyahn*
way	la direction	*lah deerehksyawn*
we	nous	*noo*
weak	faible	*fehbl*
weather	le temps	*luh tohn*
weather forecast	le bulletin météorologique	*luh bewltahn maytayoarolojheek*
wedding	les noces	*lay nos*
wedding	le mariage	*luh mahryajh*
Wednesday	mercredi	*mehrkruhdee*
week	la semaine	*lah suhmehn*
weekend	le week-end	*luh week-ehnd*
weekend duty	le service de garde	*luh sehrvees duh gahrd*
weekly ticket	l'abonnement hebdomadaire (m.)	*lahbonmohn ehbdomahdehr*
welcome	bienvenu	*byahnvuhnew*
well	bien	*byahn*
west	l'ouest (m.)	*lwehst*
wet	humide	*ewmeed*
wetsuit	la combinaison de planche à voile	*lah kawnbeenehzawn duh plohnsh ah vwahl*
what?	quoi?	*kwah?*
wheel	la roue	*lah roo*
wheelchair	la chaise roulante	*lah shehz roolohnt*
when?	quand?	*kohn?*
where?	où?	*oo?*
which?	quel?	*kehl?*
whipped cream	la crème Chantilly	*lah krehm shohnteeyee*
white	blanc	*blohn*
who?	qui?	*kee?*
wholemeal bread	le pain complet	*luh pahn kawnpleh*
why?	pourquoi?	*poorkwah?*
wide-angle lens	le grand-angle	*luh grohn tohngl*
widow	la veuve	*lah vuhv*
widower	le veuf	*luh vuhf*
wife	l'épouse (f.)	*laypooz*
wind	le vent	*luh vohn*
windbreak	le pare-vent	*luh pahrvohn*
windmill	le moulin	*luh moolahn*
window (desk)	le guichet	*luh gueesheh*
window	la fenêtre	*lah fuhnehtr*
windscreen wiper	l'essuie-glace (m.)	*lehswee glahs*

windsurf	faire de la planche	*fehr duh lah*
	à voile	*plohnsh ah vwahl*
wine	le vin	*luh vahn*
wine list	la carte des vins	*lah kahrt day vahn*
winter	l'hiver (m.)	*leevehr*
witness	le témoin	*luh taymwahn*
woman	la femme	*lah fahm*
wood	le bois	*luh bwah*
wool	la laine	*lah lehn*
word	le mot	*luh moa*
work	le travail	*luh trahvahy*
working day	le jour ouvrable	*jhoor oovrahbl*
worn	usé	*ewzay*
worried	inquiet	*ahnkyeh*
wound	la blessure	*lah blehsewr*
wrap	emballer	*ohnbahlay*
wrist	le poignet	*luh pwahnnyeh*
write	écrire	*aykreer*
write down	noter	*notay*
writing pad	le bloc-notes	*luh blok not*
writing paper	le papier à lettres	*luh pahpyay ah lehtr*
written	écrit	*aykree*
wrong	mauvais	*moaveh*

Y

yacht	le yacht	*Juh yot*
year	l'année (f.)	*lahnay*
yellow	jaune	*jhoan*
yes	oui	*wee*
yes, please	volontiers	*volawntyay*
yesterday	hier	*yehr*
yoghurt	le yaourt	*luh yahoort*
you	vous	*voo*
you too	de même	*duh mehm*
youth hostel	l'auberge de	*loabehrjh duh*
	jeunesse (f.)	*jhuhnehs*

Z

| zip | la fermeture éclair | *lah fehrmuhtewr ayklehr* |
| zoo | le parc zoologique | *luh pahrk zoaolojheek* |

Basic grammar

1 The article

French nouns are divided into 2 categories: masculine and feminine. The definite article (the) is **le,la** or **l'**:

le is used before masculine words starting with a consonant, **le magasin** (the shop)

la is used with feminine words starting with a consonant, **la plage** (the beach)

l' is used before masculine and feminine words starting with a vowel, **l'argent** (the money), **l'assiette** (the plate).

Other examples are:

le toit	the roof
la maison	the house
l'hôtel (m.)	the hotel
l'entrée (f.)	the entrance

in the case of the indefinite article (**a, an**):

un is used before masculine words, **un livre** (a book)

une is used before feminine words, **une pomme** (an apple)

des is used before plural words, both masculine and feminine, **des camions** (lorries), **des voitures** (cars).

Other examples are:

un père	a father	**une mère**	a mother
un homme	a man	**une femme**	a woman
des hommes	men	**des femmes**	women

2 The plural

The plural of **le, la** and **l'** is **les**.

The plural of most French nouns ends in **s**, but this **s** is not pronounced. However when the noun begins with a vowel or a silent **h**, then the **s** of **les** or **des** is pronounced z, **les affaires** (*layzahfehr*), **des enfants** (*dayzohngfohn*).

Other examples are:

le lit	*luh lee*	**les lits**	*lay lee*
la table	*lah tahbl*	**les tables**	*lay tahbl*
l'avion (m.)	*lahveeawn*	**les avions**	*layzahvyeeawn*
l'heure (f.)	*luhr*	**les heures**	*layzuhr*

Certain plurals end in **aux** (mainly words ending in **'al'**)

le cheval	**les chevaux**
le canal	**les canaux**

3 Personal pronouns

I	**je**
You	**tu**
He/she/it	**il/elle**
We	**nous**
You	**vous**
They	**ils/elles**

In general '**tu**' is used to translate 'you' when speaking to close friends, relatives and children. **Vous** is used in all other cases. 'It' becomes **il** or **elle** according to whether the noun referred to is masculine or feminine.

4 Possessive pronouns

	masculine	feminine	plural
my	**mon**	**ma**	**mes**
your	**ton**	**ta**	**tes**
his/her/its	**son**	**sa**	**ses**
our	**notre**	**notre**	**nos**
your	**votre**	**votre**	**vos**
their	**leur**	**leur**	**leurs**

They agree with the object they refer to, e.g. her hat = **son chapeau**.

5 Verbs

parler		to speak
je parle	root + -e	I speak
tu parles	root + -es	you speak
il/elle parle	root + -e	he/she/it speaks
nous parlons	root + -ons	we speak
vous parlez	root + -ez	you speak
ils/elles parlent	root + -ent	they speak
parlé (past participle)		spoken

Here are some useful verbs.

être	to be
je suis	I am
tu es	you are
il/elle est	he/she/it is
nous sommes	we are
vous êtes	you are
ils/elles sont	they are
été (past participle)	been

avoir	to have
j'ai	I have
tu as	you have
il/elle a	he/she/it has
nous avons	we have
vous avez	you have
ils/elles ont	they have
eu (past participle)	had

faire	to do/make
je fais	I do
tu fais	you do
il/elle fait	he/she does
nous faisons	we do
vous faites	you do
ils/elles font	they do
fait (past participle)	done/made

6 Countries and prepositions

Names of countries take the article:

L'Angleterre	England
Le Canada	Canada
La France	France

in Paris	**à Paris**
in France	**en France**
in Canada	**au Canada**

7 Negatives

Negatives are formed by using:

ne (verb) **pas**	not
ne (verb) **jamais**	never

Je ne parle pas français.	I don't speak French.
Je ne fume jamais.	I never smoke.